RUDYARD KIPLING was born on December 30, 1865, in Bombay where his father was an architectural sculptor. After a brief schooling in England, Kipling returned to India where he began a career as a journalist. While working as a reporter, he also wrote and published poems and stories, and soon gained a reputation as a writer with a fresh imagination and a vigorous style. Kipling's literary and journalistic writings brought him an enormous celebrity, and after his return to England in 1901 he continued to receive high honors and awards, among them the Nobel Prize for Literature in 1907. He died in London in 1936 and was buried in the Poet's Corner of Westminster Abbey.

"It was thick weather outside, with a rising wind. . . .
The nosing bows slapped and scuffled with the seas."

# "CAPTAINS COURAGEOUS"

## BY RUDYARD KIPLING

With an Introduction by John K. Hutchens

BANTAM PATHFINDER EDITIONS

BANTAM BOOKS / NEW YORK

*To*
JAMES CONLAND, M.D.
Brattleboro, Vermont

*I ploughed the land with horses,*
*But my heart was ill at ease,*
*For the old sea-faring men*
*Came to me now and then,*
*With their sagas of the seas.*

LONGFELLOW

$$
\text{RLI:} \quad \frac{\text{VLM} \quad 8}{\text{IL} \quad 7.10}
$$

"CAPTAINS COURAGEOUS"
*A Bantam Book / published by arrangement with*
*Doubleday & Company, Inc.*

PRINTING HISTORY
*Originally published by The Century Company, 1896*
*Doubleday edition published 1920*
*Sun Dial Young Modern edition published September 1939*
*2nd printing ..........May 1940*
*Sun Dial Regular edition published July 1937*
*2nd printing ....... November 1937*
*3rd printing ....... November 1938*
*Bantam edition published October 1946*
*New Bantam edition published September 1956*
*2nd printing ........ February 1957*
*3rd printing ........ February 1960*
*4th printing .......... October 1960*
*Bantam Classic edition published November 1960*
*6th printing ........ November 1961*
*7th printing .......... January 1962*
*Bantam Pathfinder edition published February 1963*

*Bantam Books are published by Bantam Books, Inc. Its trade-mark,*
*consisting of the words "Bantam Books" and the portrayal of a ban-*
*tam, is registered in the United States Patent Office and in other*
*countries. Marca Registrada. Printed in the United States of Amer-*
*ica. Bantam Books, Inc., 271 Madison Ave., New York 16, N. Y.*

# INTRODUCTION

As EVERYBODY knows, a writer is by no means always the best judge of his own writing. But when Rudyard Kipling called *"Captains Courageous"* a favorite of his among all his books, he was only sharing the opinion of a majority of his readers down through the years.

From its original publication in 1897 to this very day, from generation to generation, its appeal has been unfaltering—and for good reasons. It tells a lively story that invites us to turn the pages swiftly. In a broad sense it is a romantic adventure: that of a lad moving from one world to another literally in a matter of minutes. Within that romantic framework it is also an absorbingly realistic picture of a dangerous, highly skilled way of life: that of the Gloucester fishermen who once sailed their sturdy little craft from the New England coast to the Grand Banks and brought them home packed with cod and halibut.

For the men of Gloucester it was a job to be done, all in the day's work. But it was more than that, as our English visitor saw with characteristically sharp perception. Over and beyond the day's work for profit, it was a job to be done with pride and spirit.

So it really is not surprising that even those who do not greatly admire some of Kipling's other works of fiction have a special place in their hearts for this one—somewhat as those who may not like one or another of Robert Louis Stevenson's novels are unanimous in their affection for his *Treasure Island.* It may even be said that the two books rank together, and apart from all others, among seagoing tales that hold youngsters hypnotized and, as time passes, are cherished by their elders.

Re-reading *"Captains Courageous"* only recently, I was happy though not startled to see how lightly time has touched it: an out-of-date slang word lurks here and there, along with a reference to some now outmoded detail of

fashion or transportation. But absolutely nothing about it is
"quaint," as momentarily popular novels too often become
"quaint." For us, as it must have been for the very first
readers of *"Captains Courageous,"* the far-off world of the
Gloucester mariners remains new, wonderful—and timeless.
A storyteller of today could consider himself lucky if he
could be confident that his art would still live so vibrantly
a half-century hence.

One explanation for the enduringly fresh flavor of Kipling's little masterpiece might be that his methods, as a
narrative writer, are now so deeply embedded in our fiction.
Arriving in an age of leisurely "yarners," he told his stories
with a nervous speed that brought something new to English
literature. Contemporary accounts of the reception of his
earliest short stories still convey their electrifying effect. It
was impossible, people said, that so young a man could know
so much! They had not yet come to know the mind that
breathed in facts and made them its own, nor were they
aware how those near-sighted eyes, behind the thick lenses,
everywhere picked up details a very few of which did the
work of whole paragraphs in the prose of others. They
would learn later that on the other side of the world, in
India, he had begun as a newspaper reporter whose stock-
in-trade was reality. In his way he remained a reporter, and
a great one, all his life.

Solemn pundits have noted that *"Captains Courageous"*
is not so much a novel as a long short story. One who early
read it as a what-happens-next adventure, and later as a
notable example of the storyteller's art, begs to disagree.
After all, much more happens here than a short story, even
an enlarged short story, is likely to contain. A spoiled, rich
boy is suddenly separated from a transatlantic liner; is
rescued from what would have been certain death; briefly
rebels against an environment unlike anything he has known;
is won over to it, as his new friends on the schooner *We're
Here* are won over to him, when he proves his mettle.

If a novel is a narrative in which character changes and
develops with time, and is shaped by incident, surely we
have here the stuff of a novel. *"Captains Courageous"* seems
even shorter than it actually is because, I suspect, it moves at

so swift a pace and with such economy. In short, it is Kiplingesque. Where a windy writer might have taken a hundred pages to tell us that Harvey Cheyne as we first see him is an objectionable lad, and why, Kipling requires only six. Three pages beyond that, the cocky Harvey is aboard the *We're Here,* and presently is confronting that excellent skipper and philosopher, Disko Troop, who considerately punches him on the nose and sets him on the road to his coming of age.

If the plot of *"Captains Courageous"* has a fault, it is that we know too soon that the personality of Harvey Cheyne will be transformed. Otherwise, those not yet familiar with the story would be told less about it than they are learning here. Yet Kipling keeps its interest high and forward-looking throughout. It takes a kind of magic to do that, the magic consisting in this case of the true storyteller's feeling for character, the natural observer's never-ending obsession with what makes the world go round.

In the particular world that attracted Kipling in *"Captains Courageous"* the characters are a fascinatingly varied lot—arbitrarily so, it has been said, but those who say so apparently do not appreciate how men of many races and origins met as a matter of course in Gloucester in other days and went to the Grand Banks for money and, yes, for glory. A crew as mixed as the *We're Here*'s Irish Long Jack, the Portuguese Manuel, the Pennsylvania farmer Salters, and the Negro cook who swears in Gaelic, was known to every New England waterfront. As usual, the observant Kipling knew what he was doing.

Small wonder, then, that midway in his four-year American stay in the 1890s he sensed a story awaiting him in the lives of these rugged, colorful men. With the reticence that marks his book of memoirs, *Something About Myself,* he notes casually that he had gone "once or twice to Gloucester," and had attended the annual memorial service there for the men of Gloucester who had been lost at sea, before he embarked on the "little book" that turned out to be this one. With a tour of Boston harbor, his research—as he would not have called it—totaled fourteen days. This, in addition to stories that had been told him by a Vermont doctor-friend who long before had worked in the Gloucester fleet, was enough. He put aside work on *Kim*. "It grows under my hand," he said happily of his newly launched tale.

And surely we can sense his pleasure in it as he wrote—the old journalist's satisfaction in details precisely recorded, the artist's satisfaction in those details put to creative use. Scene after scene sticks in the mind: the neophyte fisherman Harvey learning to swing a fish-laden dory aboard the schooner in a rough sea, the stories and songs by night in the cabin of the *We're Here,* the long night watches as the schooner roamed over the watery prairie, the jocular rivalry with other ships from the home port, the dash for Gloucester under full sail when the work was done.

At first glance this tale of a rough, simple life seems far from the exotic background of the prose and poems with which Kipling had made his reputation virtually overnight a few years before. Yet in a basic sense *"Captains Courageous"* is of their company. For his Gloucester fishermen, like his soldiers and engineers and pioneers in far corners of the world, lived by a code. Today we may smile—and Kipling's critics sneer—at the Empire builders, their ritualistic manners and stiff-upper-lip discipline. So, occasionally, did Kipling. What he steadily, passionately admired was heroism, the unself-conscious sense of duty that meets the challenge of crisis and comes through, whether it is in a Roman centurion in ancient Britain, a Tommy Atkins in the Soudan, or a Gloucester fisherman off the Grand Banks. And who is to say that this is not a great theme, regardless of how fashions may change elsewhere in fiction? "The heroic conception of life," André Maurois has called this fundamental vision of Kipling's. Character mattered to him. Character in action, portrayed as he alone in his time could portray it, was the cornerstone of his dazzling artistry—as the pages that follow attest.

JOHN K. HUTCHENS

# CHAPTER I

THE WEATHER door of the smoking-room had been left open to the North Atlantic fog, as the big liner rolled and lifted, whistling to warn the fishing-fleet.

"That Cheyne boy's the biggest nuisance aboard," said a man in a frieze overcoat, shutting the door with a bang. "He is n't wanted here. He 's too fresh."

A white-haired German reached for a sandwich, and grunted between bites: "I know der breed. Ameriga is full of dot kind. I dell you you should imbort ropes' ends free under your dariff."

"Pshaw! There is n't any real harm to him. He 's more to be pitied than anything," a man from New York drawled, as he lay at full length along the cushions under the wet skylight. "They 've dragged him around from hotel to hotel ever since he was a kid. I was talking to his mother this morning. She 's a lovely lady, but she don't pretend to manage him. He 's going to Europe to finish his education."

"Education is n't begun yet." This was a Philadelphian, curled up in a corner. "That boy gets two hundred a month pocket-money, he told me. He is n't sixteen either."

"Railroads, his father, aind't it?" said the German.

"Yep. That and mines and lumber and shipping. Built one place at San Diego, the old man has; another at Los Angeles; owns half a dozen railroads, half the lumber on the Pacific slope, and lets his wife spend the money," the Philadelphian went on lazily. "The West don't suit her, she says. She just tracks around with the boy and her nerves, trying to find out what 'll amuse *him,* I guess. Florida, Adirondacks, Lakewood, Hot Springs, New York, and round again. He is n't much more than a second-hand hotel clerk now. When he 's finished in Europe he 'll be a holy terror."

"What 's the matter with the old man attending to him personally?" said a voice from the frieze ulster.

1

"Old man 's piling up the rocks. 'Don't want to be disturbed, I guess. He 'll find out his error a few years from now. 'Pity, because there 's a heap of good in the boy if you could get at it."

"Mit a rope's end; mit a rope's end!" growled the German.

Once more the door banged, and a slight, slim-built boy perhaps fifteen years old, a half-smoked cigarette hanging from one corner of his mouth, leaned in over the high footway. His pasty yellow complexion did not show well on a person of his years, and his look was a mixture of irresolution, bravado, and very cheap smartness. He was dressed in a cherry-coloured blazer, knickerbockers, red stockings, and bicycle shoes, with a red flannel cap at the back of the head. After whistling between his teeth, as he eyed the company, he said in a loud, high voice: "Say, it 's thick outside. You can hear the fish-boats squawking all around us. Say, would n't it be great if we ran down one?"

"Shut the door, Harvey," said the New Yorker. "Shut the door and stay outside. You 're not wanted here."

"Who 'll stop me?" he answered, deliberately. "Did *you* pay for my passage, Mister Martin? 'Guess I've as good right here as the next man."

He picked up some dice from a checker-board and began throwing, right hand against left.

"Say, gen'elmen, this is deader 'n mud. Can't we make a game of poker between us?"

There was no answer, and he puffed his cigarette, swung his legs, and drummed on the table with rather dirty fingers. Then he pulled out a roll of bills as if to count them.

"How 's your mama this afternoon?" a man said. "I did n't see her at lunch."

"In her state-room, I guess. She 's 'most always sick on the ocean. I 'm going to give the stewardess fifteen dollars for looking after her. I don't go down more 'n I can avoid. It makes me feel mysterious to pass that butler's-pantry place. Say, this is the first time I 've been on the ocean."

"Oh, don't apologize, Harvey."

"Who 's apologizing? This is the first time I 've crossed

the ocean gen'elmen, and, except the first day, I have n't been sick one little bit. *No,* sir!" He brought down his fist with a triumphant bang, wetted his finger, and went on counting the bills.

"Oh, you 're a high-grade machine, with the writing in plain sight," the Philadelphian yawned. "You 'll blossom into a credit to your country if you don't take care."

"I know it. I 'm an American—first, last, and all the time. I'll show 'em that when I strike Europe. Pff! My cig 's out. I can't smoke the truck the steward sells. Any gen'elman got a real Turkish cig on him?"

The chief engineer entered for a moment, red, smiling, and wet. "Say, Mac," cried Harvey cheerfully, "how are we hitting it?"

"Vara much in the ordinary way," was the grave reply. "The young are as polite as ever to their elders, an' their elders are e'en tryin' to appreciate it."

A low chuckle came from a corner. The German opened his cigar-case and handed a skinny black cigar to Harvey.

"Dot is der broper apparatus to smoke, my young friendt," he said. "You vill dry it? Yes? Den you vill be efer so happy."

Harvey lit the unlovely thing with a flourish: he felt that he was getting on in grown-up society.

"It would take more 'n this to keel me over," he said, ignorant that he was lighting that terrible article, a Wheeling "stogie."

"Dot we shall bresently see," said the German. "Where are we now, Mr. Mactonal'?"

"Just there or thereabouts, Mr. Schaefer," said the engineer. "We 'll be on the Grand Bank to-night; but in a general way o' speakin', we 're all among the fishing-fleet now. We 've shaved three dories an' near skelped the boom off a Frenchman since noon, an' that's close sailin', ye may say."

"You like my cigar, eh?" the German asked, for Harvey's eyes were full of tears.

"Fine, full flavour," he answered through shut teeth. "Guess we 've slowed down a little, have n't we? I 'll skip out and see what the log says."

"I might if I vhas you," said the German.

Harvey staggered over the wet decks to the nearest rail.

He was very unhappy; but he saw the deck-steward lashing chairs together, and, since he had boasted before the man that he was never seasick, his pride made him go aft to the second-saloon deck at the stern, which was finished in a turtle-back. The deck was deserted, and he crawled to the extreme end of it, near the flag-pole. There he doubled up in limp agony, for the Wheeling "stogie" joined with the surge and jar of the screw to sieve out his soul. His head swelled; sparks of fire danced before his eyes; his body seemed to lose weight, while his heels wavered in the breeze. He was fainting from seasickness, and a roll of the ship tilted him over the rail on to the smooth lip of the turtle-back. Then a low, gray mother-wave swung out of the fog, tucked Harvey under one arm, so to speak, and pulled him off and away to leeward; the great green closed over him, and he went quietly to sleep.

He was roused by the sound of a dinner-horn such as they used to blow at a summer-school he had once attended in the Adirondacks. Slowly he remembered that he was Harvey Cheyne, drowned and dead in mid-ocean, but was too weak to fit things together. A new smell filled his nostrils; wet and clammy chills ran down his back, and he was helplessly full of salt water. When he opened his eyes, he perceived that he was still on the top of the sea, for it was running round him in silver-coloured hills, and he was lying on a pile of half-dead fish, looking at a broad human back clothed in a blue jersey.

"It 's no good," thought the boy. "I 'm dead, sure enough, and this thing is in charge."

He groaned, and the figure turned its head, showing a pair of little gold rings half hidden in curly black hair.

"Aha! You feel some pretty well now?" it said. "Lie still so: we trim better."

With a swift jerk he sculled the flickering boat-head on to a foamless sea that lifted her twenty full feet, only to slide her into a glassy pit beyond. But this mountain-climbing did not interrupt blue-jersey's talk. "Fine good job, I say, that I catch you. Eh, wha-at? Better good job, I say, your boat not catch me. How you come to fall out?"

"I was sick," said Harvey; "sick, and could n't help it."

"Just in time I blow my horn, and your boat she yaw a little. Then I see you come all down. Eh, wha-at? I think you are cut into baits by the screw, but you dreeft—dreeft to me, and I make a big fish of you. So you shall not die this time."

"Where am I?" said Harvey, who could not see that life was particularly safe where he lay.

"You are with me in the dory—Manuel my name, and I come from schooner *We 're Here* of Gloucester. I live to Gloucester. By-and-by we get supper. Eh, wha-at?"

He seemed to have two pairs of hands and a head of cast-iron, for, not content with blowing through a big conch-shell, he must needs stand up to it, swaying with the sway of the flat-bottomed dory, and send a grinding, thuttering shriek through the fog. How long this entertainment lasted, Harvey could not remember, for he lay back terrified at the sight of the smoking swells. He fancied he heard a gun and a horn and shouting. Something bigger than the dory, but quite as lively, loomed alongside. Several voices talked at once; he was dropped into a dark, heaving hole, where men in oilskins gave him a hot drink and took off his clothes, and he fell asleep.

When he waked he listened for the first breakfast-bell on the steamer, wondering why his state-room had grown so small. Turning, he looked into a narrow, triangular cave, lit by a lamp hung against a huge square beam. A three-cornered table within arm's reach ran from the angle of the bows to the foremast. At the after end, behind a well-used Plymouth stove, sat a boy about his own age, with a flat red face and a pair of twinkling gray eyes. He was dressed in a blue jersey and high rubber boots. Several pairs of the same sort of foot-wear, an old cap, and some worn-out woollen socks lay on the floor, and black and yellow oilskins swayed to and fro beside the bunks. The place was packed as full of smells as a bale is of cotton. The oilskins had a peculiarly thick flavour of their own which made a sort of background to the smells of fried fish, burnt grease, paint, pepper, and stale tobacco; but these, again, were all hooped together by one encircling smell of ship and salt water. Harvey saw with disgust that there were no sheets on his bed-place. He was lying on a piece of dingy ticking full of lumps and nubbles. Then, too, the boat's motion was not that of a steamer. She was neither sliding nor rolling, but rather wriggling herself about in a silly, aimless way, like a colt at the end of a halter. Water-noises ran by close to his ear, and beams creaked and whined about him. All these things made him grunt despairingly and think of his mother.

"Feelin' better?" said the boy, with a grin. "Hev some coffee?" He brought a tin cup full and sweetened it with molasses.

"Is n't there milk?" said Harvey, looking round the dark double tier of bunks as if he expected to find a cow there.

"Well, no," said the boy. "Ner there ain't likely to be till 'baout mid-September. 'Tain't bad coffee. I made it."

Harvey drank in silence, and the boy handed him a plate full of pieces of crisp fried pork, which he ate ravenously.

"I 've dried your clothes. Guess they've shrunk some," said the boy. "They ain't our style much—none of 'em. Twist round an' see ef you 're hurt any."

Harvey stretched himself in every direction, but could not report any injuries.

"That 's good," the boy said heartily. "Fix yerself an' go on deck. Dad wants to see you. I 'm his son,—Dan, they call me,—an' I 'm cook's helper an' everything else aboard that 's too dirty for the men. There ain't no boy here 'cep' me sence Otto went overboard—an' he was only a Dutchy, an' twenty year old at that. How'd you come to fall off in a dead flat ca'am?"

"'T was n't a calm," said Harvey, sulkily. "It was a gale, and I was seasick. Guess I must have rolled over the rail."

"There was a little common swell yes'day an' last night," said the boy. "But ef thet 's your notion of a gale——" He whistled. "You 'll know more 'fore you 're through. Hurry! Dad 's waitin'."

Like many other unfortunate young people, Harvey had never in all his life received a direct order—never, at least, without long, and sometimes tearful, explanations of the advantages of obedience and the reasons for the request. Mrs. Cheyne lived in fear of breaking his spirit, which, perhaps, was the reason that she herself walked on the edge of nervous prostration. He could not see why he should be expected to hurry for any man's pleasure, and said so. "Your dad can come down here if he 's so anxious to talk to me. I want him to take me to New York right away. It 'll pay him."

Dan opened his eyes as the size and beauty of this joke dawned on him. "Say, Dad!" he shouted up the foc'sle hatch, "he says you kin slip down an' see him ef you 're anxious that way. 'Hear, Dad?"

The answer came back in the deepest voice Harvey had ever heard from a human chest: "Quit foolin', Dan, and send him to me."

Dan sniggered, and threw Harvey his warped bicycle shoes. There was something in the tones on the deck that made the boy dissemble his extreme rage and console himself with the thought of gradually unfolding the tale of his own and his father's wealth on the voyage home. This rescue would certainly make him a hero among his friends for life. He hoisted himself on deck up a perpendicular ladder, and stumbled aft, over a score of obstructions, to where a small, thick-set, clean-shaven man with gray eyebrows sat on a step that led up to the quarterdeck. The swell had passed in the night, leaving a long, oily sea, dotted round the horizon with the sails of a dozen fishing-boats. Between them lay little black specks, showing where the dories were out fishing. The schooner, with a triangular riding-sail on the mainmast, played easily at anchor, and except for the man by the cabin-roof—"house" they call it—she was deserted.

"Mornin'—Good afternoon, I should say. You 've nigh slep' the clock around, young feller," was the greeting.

"Mornin'," said Harvey. He did not like being called "young feller"; and, as one rescued from drowning, expected sympathy. His mother suffered agonies whenever he got his feet wet; but this mariner did not seem excited.

"Naow let 's hear all abaout it. It 's quite providential, first an' last, fer all concerned. What might be your name? Where from (we mistrust it 's Noo York), an' where baound (we mistrust it 's Europe)?"

Harvey gave his name, the name of the steamer, and a short history of the accident, winding up with a demand to be taken back immediately to New York, where his father would pay anything any one chose to name.

"H'm," said the shaven man, quite unmoved by the end

of Harvey's speech. "I can't say we think special of any man, or boy even, that falls overboard from that kind o' packet in a flat ca'am. Least of all when his excuse is that he 's seasick."

"Excuse!" cried Harvey. "D' you suppose I 'd fall overboard into your dirty little boat for fun?"

"Not knowin' what your notions o' fun may be, I can't rightly say, young feller. But if I was you, I would n't call the boat which, under Providence, was the means o' savin' ye, names. In the first place, it 's blame irreligious. In the second, it 's annoyin' to my feelin's—an' I 'm Disko Troop o' the We 're Here o' Gloucester, which you don't seem rightly to know."

"I don't know and I don't care," said Harvey. "I 'm grateful enough for being saved and all that, of course! but I want you to understand that the sooner you take me back to New York the better it 'll pay you."

"Meanin'—haow?" Troop raised one shaggy eyebrow over a suspiciously mild blue eye.

"Dollars and cents," said Harvey, delighted to think that he was making an impression. "Cold dollars and cents." He thrust a hand into a pocket, and threw out his stomach a little, which was his way of being grand. "You 've done the best day's work you ever did in your life when you pulled me in. I 'm all the son Harvey Cheyne has."

"He 's bin favoured," said Disko, dryly.

"And if you don't know who Harvey Cheyne is, you don't know much—that 's all. Now turn her around and let 's hurry."

Harvey had a notion that the greater part of America was filled with people discussing and envying his father's dollars.

"Mebbe I do, an' mebbe I don't. Take a reef in your stummick, young feller. It 's full o' my vittles."

Harvey heard a chuckle from Dan, who was pretending to be busy by the stump-foremast, and the blood rushed to his face. "We 'll pay for that too," he said. "When do you suppose we shall get to New York?"

"I don't use Noo York any. Ner Boston. We may see Eastern Point about September; an' your pa—I 'm real sorry I hain't heerd tell of him—may give me ten dollars efter all your talk. Then o' course he may n't."

"Ten dollars! Why, see here, I——" Harvey dived into his pocket for the wad of bills. All he brought up was a soggy packet of cigarettes.

"Not lawful currency, an' bad for the lungs. Heave 'em overboard, young feller, and try agin."

"It 's been stolen!" cried Harvey, hotly.

"You 'll hev to wait till you see your pa to reward me, then?"

"A hundred and thirty-four dollars—all stolen," said Harvey, hunting wildly through his pockets. "Give them back."

A curious change flitted across old Troop's hard face. "What might *you* have been doin' at your time o' life with with one hundred an' thirty-four dollars, young feller?"

"It was part of my pocket-money—for a month." This Harvey thought would be knock-down blow, and it was —indirectly.

"Oh! One hundred and thirty-four dollars is only part of his pocket-money—for one month only! You don't remember hittin' anything when you fell over, do you? Crack agin a stanchion, le' 's say. Old man Hasken o' the *East Wind*"—Troop seemed to be talking to himself—"he tripped on a hatch an' butted the mainmast with his head —hardish. 'Baout three weeks afterwards, old man Hasken he would hev it that the *East Wind* was a commerce-destroyin' man-o'-war, an' so he declared war on Sable Island because it was Bridish, an' the shoals run aout too far. They sewed him up in a bed-bag, his head an' feet appearin', fer the rest o' the trip, an' now he 's to home in Essex playin' with little rag dolls."

Harvey choked with rage, but Troop went on consolingly: "We 're sorry fer you. We 're very sorry fer you— an' so young. We won't say no more abaout the money, I guess."

"'Course you won't. You stole it."

"Suit yourself. We stole it ef it 's any comfort to you. Naow, abaout goin' back. Allowin' we could do it, which we can't, you ain't in no fit state to go back to your home, an' *we* 've jest come on to the Banks, workin' fer our bread. *We* don't see the ha'af of a hundred dollars a month, let alone pocket-money; an' with good luck we 'll be ashore again somewheres abaout the first weeks o' September."

"But—but it 's May now, and I can't stay here doin' nothing just because you want to fish. I *can't*, I tell you!"

"Right an' jest; jest *an'* right. No one asks you to do nothin'. There 's a heap as you *can* do, for Otto he went overboard on Le Have. I mistrust he lost his grip in a gale we f'und there. Anyways, he never come back to deny it. *You 've* turned up, plain, plumb providential for all concerned. I mistrust, though, there 's ruther few things you kin do. Ain't thet so?"

"I can make it lively for you and your crowd when we get ashore," said Harvey, with a vicious nod, murmuring vague threats about "piracy," at which Troop almost—not quite—smiled.

"Excep' talk. I 'd forgot that. You ain't asked to talk more 'n you 've a mind to aboard the *We 're Here.* Keep your eyes open, an' help Dan to do ez he 's bid, an' sech-like, an' I 'll give you—you ain't wuth it, but I 'll give—ten an' a ha'af a month; say thirty-five at the end o' the trip. A little work will ease up your head, and you kin tell us all abaout your dad an' your ma an' your money efter-wards."

"She 's on the steamer," said Harvey, his eyes filling with tears. "Take me to New York at once."

"Poor woman—poor woman! When she has you back she 'll forgit it all, though. There 's eight of us on the *We 're Here,* an' ef we went back naow—it 's more 'n a thousand mile—we 'd lose the season. The men they would n't hev it, allowin' I was agreeable."

"But my father would make it all right."

"He 'd try. I don't doubt he 'd try," said Troop; "but a whole season's catch is eight men's bread; an' you 'll be better in your health when you see him in the fall. Go forward an' help Dan. It 's ten an' a ha'af a month, ez I said, an' o' course, all f'und, same ez the rest o' us."

"Do you mean I 'm to clean pots and pans and things?" said Harvey.

"An' other things. You 've no call to shout, young fel-ler."

"I won't! My father will give you enough to buy this dirty little fish-kettle"—Harvey stamped on the deck—"ten times over, if you take me to New York safe; and—and —you 're in a hundred and thirty by me, anyhow."

"Ha-ow?" said Troop, the iron face darkening.

"How? You know how, well enough. On top of all that, you want me to do menial work"—Harvey was very proud of that adjective—"till the Fall. I tell you I will *not*. You hear?"

Troop regarded the top of the mainmast with deep interest for a while, as Harvey harangued fiercely all around him.

"Hsh!" he said at last. "I 'm figurin' out my responsibilities in my own mind. It 's a matter o' jedgment."

Dan stole up and plucked Harvey by the elbow. "Don't go to tamperin' with Dad any more," he pleaded. "You 've called him a thief two or three times over, an' he don't take that from any livin' bein'."

"I won't!" Harvey almost shrieked, disregarding the advice, and still Troop meditated.

"Seems kinder unneighbourly," he said at last, his eye travelling down to Harvey. "I don't blame you, not a mite, young feller, nor you won't blame *me* when the bile 's out o' your systim. Be sure you sense what I say? Ten an' a ha'af fer second boy on the schooner—an' all found—fer to teach you *an'* fer the sake o' your health. Yes or no?"

"No!" said Harvey. "Take me back to New York or I 'll see you——"

He did not exactly remember what followed. He was lying in the scuppers, holding on to a nose that bled while Troop looked down on him serenely.

"Dan," he said to his son, "I was sot agin this young feller when I first saw him on account o' hasty jedgments. Never you be led astray by hasty jedgments, Dan. Naow I 'm sorry for him, because he 's clear distracted in his upper works. He ain't responsible fer the names he 's give me, nor fer his other statements—nor fer jumpin' overboard, which I 'm abaout ha'af convinced he did. You be gentle with him, Dan, 'r I 'll give you twice what I 've give him. Them hemmeridges clears the head. Let him sluice it off!"

Troop went down solemnly into the cabin, where he and the older men bunked, leaving Dan to comfort the luckless heir to thirty millions.

# CHAPTER II

"I WARNED ye," said Dan, as the drops fell thick and fast on the dark, oiled planking. "Dad ain't noways hasty, but you fair earned it. Pshaw! there 's no sense takin' on so." Harvey's shoulders were rising and falling in spasms of dry sobbing. "I know the feelin'. First time Dad laid me out was the last—and that was my first trip. Makes ye feel sickish an' lonesome. *I* know."

"It does," moaned Harvey. "That man 's either crazy or drunk, and—and I can't do anything."

"Don't say that to Dad," whispered Dan. "He 's set agin all liquor, an'—well, he told me *you* was the madman. What in creation made you call him a thief? He 's my dad."

Harvey sat up, mopped his nose, and told the story of the missing wad of bills. "I 'm not crazy," he wound up. "Only—your father has never seen more than a five-dollar bill at a time, and *my* father could buy up this boat once a week and never miss it."

"You don't know what the *We 're Here 's* worth. Your dad must hev a pile o' money. How did he git it? Dad sez loonies can't shake out a straight yarn. Go ahead."

"In gold mines and things, West."

"I 've read o' that kind o' business. Out West, too? Does he go around with a pistol on a trick-pony, same ez the circus? They call that the Wild West, and I 've heard that their spurs an' bridles was solid silver."

"You *are* a chump!" said Harvey, amused in spite of himself. "My father has n't any use for ponies. When he wants to ride he takes his car."

"Haow? Lobster-car?"

"No. His own private car, of course. You 've seen a private car some time in your life?"

"Slatin Beeman he hez one," said Dan, cautiously. "I saw her at the Union Depot in Boston, with three men hoggin' her run." (Dan meant cleaning the windows.)

"But Slatin Beeman he owns 'baout every railroad on Long Island, they say, an' they say he 's bought 'baout ha'af Noo Hampshire an' run a line fence around her, an' filled her up with lions an' tigers an' bears an' buffalo an' crocodiles an' such all. Slatin Beeman he's a millionaire. I 've seen *his* car. Yes?"

"Well, my father 's what they call a multimillionaire, and he has two private cars. One 's named for me, the Harvey, and one for my mother, the Constance."

"Hold on," said Dan. "Dad don't ever let me swear, but I guess *you* can. 'Fore we go ahead, I want you to say hope you may die if you 're lyin'."

"Of course," said Harvey.

"Thet ain't 'nuff. Say, 'Hope I may die if I ain't speakin' truth.'"

"Hope I may die right here," said Harvey, "if every word I 've spoken is n't the cold truth."

"Hundred an' thirty-four dollars an' all?" said Dan. "I heard ye talkin' to Dad, an' I ha'af looked you 'd be swallered up, same 's Jonah."

Harvey protested himself red in the face. Dan was a shrewd young person along his own lines, and ten minutes' questioning convinced him that Harvey was not lying—much. Besides, he had bound himself by the most terrible oath known to boyhood, and yet he sat, alive, with a red-ended nose, in the scuppers, recounting marvels upon marvels.

"Gosh!" said Dan at last from the very bottom of his soul when Harvey had completed an inventory of the car named in his honour. Then a grin of mischievous delight overspread his broad face. "I believe you, Harvey. Dad's made a mistake fer once in his life."

"He has, sure," said Harvey, who was meditating an early revenge.

"He 'll be mad clear through. Dad jest hates to be mistook in his jedgments." Dan lay back and slapped his thigh. "Oh, Harvey, don't you spile the catch by lettin' on."

"I don't want to be knocked down again. I 'll get even with him, though."

"Never heard any man ever got even with Dad. But he 'd knock ye down again sure. The more he was mistook the more he 'd do it. But gold mines *and* pistols——"

"I never said a word about pistols," Harvey cut in, for he was on his oath.

"Thet 's so; no more you did. Two private cars, then, one named fer you an' one fer her; an' two hundred dollars a month pocket-money, all knocked into the scuppers fer not workin' fer ten an' a ha'af a month! It's the top haul o' the season." He exploded with noiseless chuckles.

"Then I was right?" said Harvey, who thought he had found a sympathizer.

"You was wrong; the wrongest kind o' wrong! You take right hold an' pitch in 'longside o' me, or you 'll catch it, an' I 'll catch it fer backin' you up. Dad always gives me double helps 'cause I 'm his son, an' he hates favourin' folk. Guess you 're kinder mad at Dad. I 've been that way time an' again. But Dad 's a mighty jest man; all the Fleet says so."

"Looks like justice, this, don't it?" Harvey pointed to his outraged nose.

"Thet 's nothin'. Lets the shore blood outer you. Dad did it for yer health. Say, though, I can't have dealin's with a man that thinks me or Dad or any one on the *We 're Here 's* a thief. We ain't any common wharf-end crowd by any manner o' means. We 're fishermen, an' we 've shipped together for six years an' more. Don't you make any mistake on *that!* I told ye Dad don't let me swear. He calls 'em vain oaths, and pounds me; but ef I could say what you said 'baout your pap an' his fixin's, I'd say that 'baout your dollars. I dunno what was in your pockets when I dried your kit fer I did n't look to see; but I'd say, using the very same words ez you used just now, neither me nor Dad—an' we was the only two that teched you after you was brought aboard—knows anythin' 'baout the money. Thet 's *my* say. Naow?"

The blood letting had certainly cleared Harvey's brain, and maybe the loneliness of the sea had something to do with it. "That 's all right," he said. Then he looked down confusedly. "Seems to me that for a fellow just saved from drowning I have n't been over and above grateful, Dan."

"Well, you was shook up and silly," said Dan. "Anyway there was only Dad an' me aboard to see it. The cook he don't count."

The "We're Here."

"I might have thought about losing the bills that way," Harvey said, half to himself, "instead of calling everybody in sight a thief. Where 's your father?"

"In the cabin. What d' you want o' him again?"

"You 'll see," said Harvey, and he stepped, rather groggily, for his head was still singing, to the cabin steps where the little ship's clock hung in plain sight of the wheel. Troop, in the chocolate-and-yellow painted cabin, was busy with a note-book and an enormous black pencil which he sucked hard from time to time.

"I have n't acted quite right," said Harvey, surprised at his own meekness.

"What 's wrong naow?" said the skipper. "Walked into Dan, hev ye?"

"No; it 's about you."

"I 'm here to listen."

"Well, I—I 'm here to take things back," said Harvey very quickly. "When a man 's saved from drowning——" he gulped.

"Ey? You 'll make a man yet ef you go on this way."

"He ought n't begin by calling people names."

"Jest an' right—right an' jest," said Troop, with the ghost of a dry smile.

"So I 'm here to say I 'm sorry." Another big gulp.

Troop heaved himself slowly off the locker he was sitting on and held out an eleven-inch hand. "I mistrusted 't would do you sights o' good; an' this shows I were n't mistook in my jedgments." A smothered chuckle on deck caught his ear. "I am very seldom mistook in my jedgments." The eleven-inch hand closed on Harvey's, numbing it to the elbow. "We 'll put a little more gristle to that 'fore we 've done with you, young feller; an' I don't think any worse of ye fer anythin' thet's gone by. You was n't fairly responsible. Go right abaout your business an' you won't take no hurt."

"You 're white," said Dan, as Harvey regained the deck, flushed to the tips of his ears.

"I don't feel it," said he.

"I didn't mean that way. I heard what Dad said. When Dad allows he don't think the worse of any man, Dad 's give himself away. He hates to be mistook in his jedgments too. Ho! ho! Onct Dad has a jedgment, he 'd sooner dip

his colours to the British than change it. I 'm glad it 's
settled right eend up. Dad 's right when he says he can't
take you back. It 's all the livin' we make here—fishin'.
The men 'll be back like sharks after a dead whale in ha'af
an hour."

"What for?" said Harvey.

"Supper, o' course. Don't your stummick tell you? You 've
a heap to learn."

"Guess I have," said Harvey, dolefully, looking at the
tangle of ropes and blocks overhead.

"She's a daisy," said Dan, enthusiastically, misunder-
standing the look. "Wait till our mainsail 's bent, an' she
walks home with all her salt wet. There 's some work
first, though." He pointed down into the darkness of the
open main-hatch between the two masts.

"What 's that for? It 's all empty," said Harvey.

"You an' me an' a few more hev got to fill it," said Dan.
"That 's where the fish goes."

"Alive?" said Harvey.

"Well, no. They 're so 's to be ruther dead—an' flat—
an' salt. There 's a hundred hogshead o' salt in the bins,
an' we hain't more 'n covered our dunnage to now."

"Where are the fish, though?"

"In the sea they say, in the boats we pray," said Dan,
quoting a fisherman's proverb. "You come in last night
with 'baout forty of 'em."

He pointed to a sort of wooden pen just in front of
the quarter-deck.

"You an' me we 'll sluice that out when they 're through.
'Send we 'll hev full pens to-night! I 've seen her down
ha'af a foot with fish waitin' to clean, an' we stood to the
tables till we was splittin' ourselves instid o' them, we was
so sleepy. Yes, they 're comin' in naow." Dan looked over
the low bulwarks at half a dozen dories rowing towards
them over the shining, silky sea.

"I 've never seen the sea from so low down," said Harvey. "It 's fine."

The low sun made the water all purple and pinkish,
with golden lights on the barrels of the long swells, and
blue and green mackerel shades in the hollows. Each
schooner in sight seemed to be pulling her dories towards

her by invisible strings, and the little black figures in the tiny boats pulled like clockwork toys.

"They 've struck on good," said Dan, between his half-shut eyes. "Manuel hain't room fer another fish. Low ez a lily-pad in still water, ain't he?"

"Which is Manuel? I don't see how you can tell 'em 'way off, as you do."

"Last boat to the south'ard. He f'und you last night," said Dan, pointing. "Manuel rows Portugoosey; ye can't mistake him. East o' him—*he 's* a heap better 'n he rows—is Pennsylvania. Loaded with saleratus, by the looks of him. East o' him—see how pretty they string out all along—with the humpy shoulders, is Long Jack. He 's a Galway man inhabitin' South Boston, where they all live mostly, an' mostly them Galway men are good in a boat. North, away yonder—you 'll hear him tune up in a minute—is Tom Platt. Man-o'-war's man he was on the old *Ohio*—first of our navy, he says, to go araound the Horn. He never talks of much else, 'cept when he sings, but he has fair fishin' luck. There! What did I tell you?"

A melodious bellow stole across the water from the northern dory. Harvey heard something about somebody's hands and feet being cold, and then:

"Bring forth the chart, the doleful chart,
    See where them mountings meet!
The clouds are thick around their heads,
    The mists around their feet."

"Full boat," said Dan, with a chuckle. "If he give us 'O Captain' it 's toppin' too!"

The bellow continued:

"And naow to thee, O Capting,
    Most earnestly I pray,
That they shall never bury me
    In church or cloister gray."

"Double game for Tom Platt. He 'll tell you all about the old *Ohio* to-morrow. 'See that blue dory behind him? He 's my uncle,—Dad's own brother,—an' ef there's any bad luck loose on the Banks she 'll fetch up agin Uncle

Salters, sure. Look how tender he 's rowin'. I 'll lay my
wage and share he 's the only man stung up to-day—an'
he 's stung up good."

"What 'll sting him?" said Harvey, getting interested.

"Strawberries, mostly. Pumpkins, sometimes, an' sometimes lemons an' cucumbers. Yes, he 's stung up from his
elbows down. That man's luck 's perfectly paralyzin'. Naow
we 'll take a-holt o' the tackles an' hist 'em in. Is it true
what you told me jest now, that you never done a hand's
turn o' work in all your born life? Must feel kinder awful,
don't it?"

"I 'm going to try to work, anyway," Harvey replied
stoutly. "Only it 's all dead new."

"Lay a-holt o' that tackle, then. Behind ye!"

Harvey grabbed at a rope and long iron hook dangling
from one of the stays of the mainmast, while Dan pulled
down another that ran from something he called a "top-
ping-lift," as Manuel drew alongside in his loaded dory.
The Portuguese smiled a brilliant smile that Harvey learned
to know well later, and with a short-handled fork began to
throw fish into the pen on deck. "Two hundred and thirty-
one," he shouted.

"Give him the hook," said Dan, and Harvey ran it into
Manuel's hands. He slipped it through a loop of rope at
the dory's bow, caught Dan's tackle, hooked it to the stern-
becket, and clambered into the schooner.

"Pull!" shouted Dan, and Harvey pulled, astonished to
find how easily the dory rose.

"Hold on, she don't nest in the cross-trees!" Dan laughed;
and Harvey held on, for the boat lay in the air above his
head.

"Lower away," Dan shouted, and as Harvey lowered,
Dan swayed the light boat with one hand till it landed
softly just behind the mainmast. "They don't weigh nothin'
empty. Thet was right smart fer a passenger. There 's more
trick to it in a sea-way."

"Ah ha!" said Manuel, holding out a brown hand. "You
are some pretty well now? This time last night the fish
they fish for you. Now you fish for fish. Eh, wha-at?"

"I 'm—I 'm ever so grateful," Harvey stammered, and
his unfortunate hand stole to his pocket once more, but

he remembered that he had no money to offer. When he knew Manuel better the mere thought of the mistake he might have made would cover him with hot, uneasy blushes in his bunk.

"There is no to be thankful for to *me!*" said Manuel. "How shall I leave you dreef, dreef all around the Banks? Now you are a fisherman—eh, wha-at? Ouh! Auh!" he bent backward and forward stiffly from the hips to get the kinks out of himself.

"I have not cleaned boat to-day. Too busy. They struck on queek. Danny, my son, clean for me."

Harvey moved forward at once. Here was something he could do for the man who had saved his life.

Dan threw him a swab, and he leaned over the dory, mopping up the slime clumsily, but with great good-will. "Hike out the foot-boards; they slide in them grooves," said Dan. "Swab 'em an' lay 'em down. Never let a foot-board jam. Ye may want her bad some day. Here 's Long Jack."

A stream of glittering fish flew into the pen from a dory alongside.

"Manuel, you take the tackle. I 'll fix the tables. Harvey, clear Manuel's boat. Long Jack's nestin' on the top of her."

Harvey looked up from his swabbing at the bottom of another dory just above his head.

"Jest like the Injian puzzle-boxes, ain't they?" said Dan, as the one boat dropped into the other.

"Takes to ut like a duck to water," said Long Jack, a grizzly-chinned, long-lipped Galway man, bending to and fro exactly as Manuel had done. Disko in the cabin growled up the hatchway, and they could hear him suck his pencil.

"Wan hunder an' forty-nine an' a half—bad luck to ye, Discobolus!" said Long Jack. "I 'm murderin' meself to fill your pockuts. Slate ut for a bad catch. The Portugee has bate me."

Whack came another dory alongside, and more fish shot into the pen.

"Two hundred and three. Let 's look at the passenger!" The speaker was even larger than the Galway man, and

his face was made curious by a purple cut running slant-
ways from his left eye to the right corner of his mouth.

Not knowing what else to do, Harvey swabbed each
dory as it came down, pulled out the foot-boards, and laid
them in the bottom of the boat.

"He 's caught on good," said the scarred man, who was
Tom Platt, watching him critically. "There are two ways
o' doin' everything. One 's fisher-fashion—any end first
an' a slippery hitch over all—an' the other 's——"

"What we did on the old *Ohio!*" Dan interrupted,
brushing into the knot of men with a long board on legs.
"Get out o' here, Tom Platt, an' leave me fix the tables."

He jammed one end of the board into two nicks in the
bulwarks, kicked out the leg, and ducked just in time to
avoid a swinging blow from the man-o'-war's man.

"An' they did that on the *Ohio,* too, Danny. See?" said
Tom Platt, laughing.

"Guess they was swivel eyed, then, fer it did n't git home,
and I know who 'll find his boots on the main-truck ef he
don't leave us alone. Haul ahead! I'm busy, can't ye see?"

"Danny, ye lie on the cable an' sleep all day," said Long
Jack. "You 're the hoight av impidence, an' I 'm persuaded
ye 'll corrupt our supercargo in a week."

"His name 's Harvey," said Dan, waving two strangely
shaped knives, "an' he 'll be worth five of any Sou' Boston
clam-digger 'fore long." He laid the knives tastefully on
the table, cocked his head on one side, and admired the
effect.

"I think it 's forty-two," said a small voice overside, and
there was a roar of laughter as another voice answered,
"Then my luck 's turned fer onct, 'caze I 'm forty-five,
though I be stung outer all shape."

"Forty-two *or* forty-five. I've lost count," the small voice
said.

"It 's Penn an' Uncle Salters caountin' catch. This beats
the circus any day," said Dan. "Jest look at 'em!"

"Come in—come in!" roared Long Jack. "It 's wet out
yondher, children."

"Forty-two, ye said." This was Uncle Salters.

"I 'll count again, then," the voice replied meekly.

The two dories swung together and bunted into the
schooner's side.

"Patience o' Jerusalem!" snapped Uncle Salters, backing water with a splash. "What possest a farmer like you to set foot in a boat beats me. You 've nigh stove me all up."

"I am sorry, Mr. Salters. I came to sea on account of nervous dyspepsia. You advised me, I think."

"You an' your nervis dyspepsy be drowned in the Whalehole," roared Uncle Salters, a fat and tubby little man. "You 're comin' down on me agin. *Did* ye say forty-two or forty-five?"

"I 've forgotten, Mr. Salters. Let's count."

"Don't see as it *could* be forty-five. *I* 'm forty-five," said Uncle Salters. "You count keerful, Penn."

Disko Troop came out of the cabin. "Salters, you pitch your fish in naow at once," he said in the tone of authority.

"Don't spile the catch, Dad," Dan murmured. "Them two are on'y jest beginnin'."

"Mother av delight! He's forkin' them wan by wan," howled Long Jack, as Uncle Salters got to work laboriously; the little man in the other dory counting a line of notches on the gunwale.

"That was last week's catch," he said, looking up plaintively, his forefinger where he had left off.

Manuel nudged Dan, who darted to the after-tackle, and, leaning far overside, slipped the hook into the stern-rope as Manuel made her fast forward. The others pulled gallantly and swung the boat in—man, fish, and all.

"One, two, four—nine," said Tom Platt, counting with a practised eye. "Forty-seven. Penn, you 're it!" Dan let the after-tackle run, and slid him out of the stern on to the deck amid a torrent of his own fish.

"Hold on!" roared Uncle Salters, bobbing by the waist. "Hold on, I 'm a bit mixed in my caount."

He had no time to protest, but was hove inboard and treated like "Pennsylvania."

"Forty-one," said Tom Platt. "Beat by a farmer, Salters. An' you sech a sailor, too!"

" 'T were n't fair caount," said he, stumbling out of the pen; "an' I 'm stung up all to pieces."

His thick hands were puffy and mottled purply white.

"Some folks will find strawberry-bottom," said Dan,

addressing the newly risen moon, "ef they hev to dive fer it, seems to me."

"An' others," said Uncle Salters, "eats the fat o' the land in sloth, an' mocks their own blood-kin."

"Seat ye! Seat ye!" a voice Harvey had not heard called from the foc'sle. Disko Troop, Tom Platt, Long Jack, and Salters went forward on the word. Little Penn bent above his square deep-sea reel and the tangled cod-lines; Manuel lay down full length on the deck, and Dan dropped into the hold, where Harvey heard him banging casks with a hammer.

"Salt," he said, returning. "Soon as we 're through supper we git to dressing-down. You 'll pitch to Dad. Tom Platt an' Dad they stow together, an' you 'll hear 'em arguin'. We 're second ha'af, you an' me an' Manuel an' Penn— the youth an' beauty o' the boat."

"What 's the good of that?" said Harvey. "I 'm hungry."

"They 'll be through in a minute. Snff! She smells good to-night. Dad ships a good cook ef he *do* suffer with his brother. It 's a full catch to-day, ain't it?" He pointed at the pens piled high with cod. "What water did ye hev, Manuel?"

"Twenty-fife father," said the Portuguese, sleepily. "They strike on good an' queek. Some day I show you, Harvey."

The moon was beginning to walk on the still sea before the elder men came aft. The cook had no need to cry "second half." Dan and Manuel were down the hatch and at table ere Tom Platt, last and most deliberate of the elders, had finished wiping his mouth with the back of his hand. Harvey followed Penn, and sat down before a tin pan of cod's tongues and sounds, mixed with scraps of pork and fried potato, a loaf of hot bread, and some black and powerful coffee. Hungry as they were, they waited while "Pennsylvania" solemnly asked a blessing. Then they stoked in silence till Dan drew a breath over his tin cup and demanded of Harvey how he felt.

" 'Most full, but there 's just room for another piece."

The cook was a huge, jet-black Negro, and, unlike all the Negroes Harvey had met, did not talk, contenting himself with smiles and dumb-show invitations to eat more.

"See, Harvey," said Dan, rapping with his fork on the

table, "it 's jest as I said. The young an' handsome men
—like me an' Pennsy an' you an' Manuel—we 're second
ha'af, an' we eats when the first ha'af are through. They 're
the old fish; an' they 're mean an' humpy, an' their stum-
micks has to be humoured; so they come first, which they
don't deserve. Ain't that so, doctor?"

The cook nodded.

"Can't he talk?" said Harvey in a whisper.

"'Nough to git along. Not much o' anything we know.
His natural tongue 's kinder curious. Comes from the in-
nards of Cape Breton, he does, where the farmers speak
homemade Scotch. Cape Breton 's full o' Negroes whose
folk run in there durin' aour war, an' they talk like farmers
—all huffy-chuffy."

"That is not Scotch," said "Pennsylvania." "That is Gaelic.
So I read in a book."

"Penn reads a heap. Most of what he says is so—'cep'
when it comes to a caount o' fish—eh?"

"Does your father just let them *say* how many they 've
caught without checking them?" said Harvey.

"Why, yes. Where 's the sense of a man lyin' fer a few
old cod?"

"Was a man once lied for his catch," Manuel put in.
"Lied every day. Fife, ten, twenty-fife more fish than come
he say there was."

"Where was that?" said Dan. "None o' aour folk."

"Frenchman of Anguille."

"Ah! Them West Shore Frenchmen don't caount anyway. Stands to reason they can't caount. Ef you run acrost
any of their soft hooks, Harvey, you 'll know why," said
Dan, with an awful contempt.

> "Always more and never less,
> Every time we come to dress,"

Long Jack roared down the hatch, and the "second ha'af"
scrambled up at once.

The shadow of the masts and rigging, with the never-
furled riding-sail, rolled to and fro on the heaving deck
in the moonlight; and the pile of fish by the stern shone
like a dump of fluid silver. In the hold there were tram-
plings and rumblings where Disko Troop and Tom Platt

moved among the salt-bins. Dan passed Harvey a pitch-fork, and led him to the inboard end of the rough table, where Uncle Salters was drumming impatiently with a knife-haft. A tub of salt water lay at his feet.

"You pitch to Dad an' Tom Platt down the hatch, an' take keer Uncle Salters don't cut yer eye out," said Dan, swinging himself into the hold. "I 'll pass salt below."

Penn and Manuel stood knee deep among cod in the pen, flourishing drawn knives. Long Jack, a basket at his feet and mittens on his hands, faced Uncle Salters at the table, and Harvey stared at the pitchfork and the tub.

"Hi!" shouted Manuel, stooping to the fish, and bringing one up with a finger under its gill and a finger in its eyes. He laid it on the edge of the pen; the knife-blade glimmered with a sound of tearing, and the fish, slit from throat to vent, with a nick on either side of the neck, dropped at Long Jack's feet.

"Hi!" said Long Jack, with a scoop of his mittened hand. The cod's liver dropped in the basket. Another wrench and scoop sent the head and offal flying, and the empty fish slid across to Uncle Salters, who snorted fiercely. There was another sound of tearing, the backbone flew over the bulwarks, and the fish, headless, gutted, and open, splashed in the tub, sending the salt water into Harvey's astonished mouth. After the first yell, the men were silent. The cod moved along as though they were alive, and long ere Harvey had ceased wondering at the miraculous dexterity of it all, his tub was full.

"Pitch!" grunted Uncle Salters, without turning his head, and Harvey pitched the fish by twos and threes down the hatch.

"Hi! Pitch 'em bunchy," shouted Dan. "Don't scatter! Uncle Salters is the best splitter in the fleet. Watch him mind his book!"

Indeed, it looked a little as though the round uncle were cutting magazine pages against time. Manuel's body, cramped over from the hips, stayed like a statue; but his long arms grabbed the fish without ceasing. Little Penn toiled valiantly, but it was easy to see he was weak. Once or twice Manuel found time to help him without breaking the chain of supplies, and once Manuel howled because he had caught his finger in a Frenchman's hook. These hooks are made of soft metal, to be rebent after use; but the cod very often get away with them and are hooked again elsewhere; and that is one of the many reasons why the Gloucester boats despise the Frenchmen.

Down below, the rasping sound of rough salt rubbed on rough flesh sounded like the whirring of a grindstone—a steady undertune to the "click-nick" of knives in the pen; the wrench and shloop of torn heads, dropped liver, and flying offal; the "caraaah" of Uncle Salters' knife scooping away backbones; and the flap of wet, open bodies falling into the tub.

At the end of an hour Harvey would have given the world to rest; for fresh, wet cod weigh more than you would think, and his back ached with the steady pitching. But he felt for the first time in his life that he was one of the working gang of men, took pride in the thought, and held on sullenly.

"Knife oh!" shouted Uncle Salters at last. Penn doubled up, gasping among the fish, Manuel bowed back and forth to supple himself, and Long Jack leaned over the bulwarks. The cook appeared, noiseless as a black shadow, collected a mass of backbones and heads, and retreated.

"Blood-ends for breakfast an' head-chowder," said Long Jack, smacking his lips.

"Knife oh!" repeated Uncle Salters, waving the flat, curved splitter's weapon.

"Look by your foot, Harve," cried Dan below.

Harvey saw half a dozen knives stuck in a cleat in the hatch combing. He dealt these around, taking over the dulled ones.

"Water!" said Disko Troop.

"Scuttle-butt 's for'ard an' the dipper 's alongside. Hurry, Harve," said Dan.

He was back in a minute with a big dipperful of stale brown water which tasted like nectar, and loosed the jaws of Disko and Tom Platt.

"These are cod," said Disko. "They ain't Damarskus figs, Tom Platt, nor yet silver bars. I 've told you that every single time since we 've sailed together."

"A matter o' seven seasons," returned Tom Platt coolly.

"Good stowin 's good stowin' all the same, an' there 's a
right an' a wrong away o' stowin' ballast even. If you 'd
ever seen four hundred ton o' iron set into the——"

"Hi!" With a yell from Manuel the work began again,
and never stopped till the pen was empty. The instant the
last fish was down, Disko Troop rolled aft to the cabin
with his brother; Manuel and Long Jack went forward; Tom
Platt only waited long enough to slide home the hatch ere
he too disappeared. In half a minute Harvey heard deep
snores in the cabin, and he was staring blankly at Dan and
Penn.

"I did a little better that time, Danny," said Penn, whose
eyelids were heavy with sleep. "But I think it is my duty
to help clean."

" 'Would n't hev your conscience fer a thousand quintal," said Dan. "Turn in, Penn. You 've no call to do boy's
work. Draw a bucket, Harvey. Oh, Penn, dump these in the
gurry-butt 'fore you sleep. Kin you keep awake that long?"

Penn took up the heavy basket of fish-livers, emptied
them into a cask with a hinged top lashed by the foc'sle;
then he too dropped out of sight in the cabin.

"Boys clean up after dressin' down, an' first watch in
ca'am weather is boy's watch on the *We 're Here.*" Dan
sluiced the pen energetically, unshipped the table, set it
up to dry in the moonlight, ran the red knife-blades through
a wad of oakum, and began to sharpen them on a tiny
grindstone, as Harvey threw offal and backbones overboard
under his direction.

At the first splash a silvery-white ghost rose bolt up-
right from the oily water and sighed a weird whistling
sigh. Harvey started back with a shout, but Dan only
laughed. "Grampus," said he. "Beggin' fer fish-heads. They
up-eend thet way when they 're hungry. Breath on him
like the doleful tombs, hain't he?" A horrible stench of
decayed fish filled the air as the pillar of white sank, and
the water bubbled oilily. "Hain't ye never seen a grampus
up-eend before? You 'll see 'em by hundreds 'fore ye 're
through. Say, it 's good to hev a boy aboard again. Otto was
too old, an' a Dutchy at that. Him an' me we fought consid'ble. 'Would n't ha' keered fer that ef he'd hed a Chris-
tian tongue in his head. Sleepy?"

"Dead sleepy," said Harvey, nodding forward.

"Must n't sleep on watch. Rouse up an' see ef our anchor-light 's bright an' shinin'. You 're on watch now, Harve."

"Pshaw! What 's to hurt us? 'Bright 's day. Sn—orrr!"

"Jest when things happen, Dad says. Fine weather 's good sleepin', an' 'fore you know, mebbe, you 're cut in two by a liner, an' seventeen brass-bound officers, all gen'elmen, lift their hand to it that your lights was aout an' there was a thick fog. Harve, I 've kinder took to you, but ef you nod onct more I 'll lay into you with a rope's end."

The moon, who sees many strange things on the Banks, looked down on a slim youth in knickerbockers and a red jersey, staggering around the cluttered decks of a seventy-ton schooner, while behind him, waving a knotted rope, walked, after the manner of an executioner, a boy who yawned and nodded between the blows he dealt.

The lashed wheel groaned and kicked softly, the riding-sail slatted a little in the shifts of the light wind, the windlass creaked, and the miserable procession continued. Harvey expostulated, threatened, whimpered, and at last wept outright, while Dan, the words clotting on his tongue, spoke of the beauty of watchfulness and slashed away with the rope's end, punishing the dories as often as he hit Harvey. At last the clock in the cabin struck ten, and upon the tenth stroke little Penn crept on deck. He found two boys in two tumbled heaps side by side on the main hatch, so deeply asleep that he actually rolled them to their berths.

# CHAPTER III

IT WAS the forty-fathom slumber that clears the soul and eye and heart, and sends you to breakfast ravening. They emptied a big tin dish of juicy fragments of fish—the blood-ends the cook had collected overnight. They cleaned up the plates and pans of the elder mess, who were out fishing, sliced pork for the midday meal, swabbed down the foc'sle, filled the lamps, drew coal and water for the cook, and investigated the fore-hold, where the boat's stores were stacked. It was another perfect day—soft, mild, and clear; and Harvey breathed to the very bottom of his lungs.

More schooners had crept up in the night, and the long blue seas were full of sails and dories. Far away on the horizon, the smoke of some liner, her hull invisible, smudged the blue, and to eastward a big ship's tog-gallant sails, just lifting, made a square nick in it. Disko Troop was smoking by the roof of the cabin—one eye on the craft around, and the other on the little fly at the main-mast-head.

"When Dad kerflummoxes that way," said Dan in a whisper, "he's doin' some high-line thinkin' fer all hands. I 'll lay my wage an' share we 'll make berth soon. Dad he knows the cod, an' the Fleet they know Dad knows. 'See 'em comin' up one by one, lookin' fer nothin' in particular, o' course, but scrowgin' on us all the time? There's the *Prince Leboo;* she's a Chat-ham boat. She's crep' up sence last night. An' see that big one with a patch in her foresail an' a new jib? She's the *Carrie Pitman* from West Chat-ham. She won't keep her canvas long onless her luck 's changed since last season. She don't do much 'cep' drift. There ain't an anchor made 'll hold her. . . . When the smoke puffs up in little rings like that, Dad's studyin' the fish. Ef we speak to him now, he'll git mad. Las' time I did, he jest took an' hove a boot at me."

Disko Troop stared forward, the pipe between his teeth, with eyes that saw nothing. As his son said, he was studying

30

the fish—pitting his knowledge and experience on the Banks against the roving cod in his own sea. He accepted the presence of the inquisitive schooners on the horizon as a compliment to his powers. But now that it was paid, he wished to draw away and make his berth alone, till it was time to go up to the Virgin and fish in the streets of that roaring town upon the waters. So Disko Troop thought of recent weather, and gales, currents, food-supplies, and other domestic arrangements, from the point of view of a twenty-pound cod; was, in fact, for an hour a cod himself, and looked remarkably like one. Then he removed the pipe from his teeth.

"Dad," said Dan, "we've done our chores. Can't we go overside a piece? It's good catchin' weather."

"Not in that cherry-coloured rig ner them ha'af baked brown shoes. Give him suthin' fit to wear."

"Dad's pleased—that settles it," said Dan, delightedly, dragging Harvey into the cabin, while Troop pitched a key down the steps. "Dad keeps my spare rig where he kin overhaul it, 'cause Ma sez I'm keerless." He rummaged through a locker, and in less than three minutes Harvey was adorned with fisherman's rubber boots that came half up his thigh, a heavy blue jersey well darned at the elbows, a pair of nippers, and a sou'wester.

"Naow ye look somethin' like," said Dan. "Hurry!"

"Keep nigh an' handy," said Troop, "an' don't go visitin' raound the Fleet. If any one asks you what I'm cal'latin to do, speak the truth—fer ye don't know."

A little red dory, labelled *Hattie S.,* lay astern of the schooner. Dan hauled in the painter, and dropped lightly on to the bottom boards, while Harvey tumbled clumsily after.

"That's no way o' gettin' into a boat," said Dan. "Ef there was any sea you'd go to the bottom, sure. You got to learn to meet her."

Dan fitted the thole-pins, took the forward thwart and watched Harvey's work. The boy had rowed, in a lady-like fashion, on the Adirondack ponds; but there is a difference between squeaking pins and well-balanced rullocks—light sculls and stubby, eight-foot sea-oars. They stuck in the gentle swell, and Harvey grunted.

"Short! Row short!" said Dan. "Ef you cramp your oar

in any kind o' sea you 're liable to turn her over. Ain't she
a daisy? Mine, too."

The little dory was specklessly clean. In her bows lay a
tiny anchor, two jugs of water, and some seventy fathoms
of thin, brown dory-roding. A tin dinner-horn rested in
cleats just under Harvey's right hand, beside an ugly-look-
ing maul, a short gaff, and a shorter wooden stick. A
couple of lines, with very heavy leads and double cod-
hooks, all neatly coiled on square reels, were stuck in their
place by the gunwale.

"Where 's the sail and mast?" said Harvey, for his
hands were beginning to blister.

Dan chuckled. "Ye don't sail fishin'-dories much. Ye
pull; but ye need n't pull so hard. Don't you wish you
owned her?"

"Well, I guess my father might give me one or two if I
asked 'im," Harvey replied. He had been too busy to
think much of his family till then.

"That's so. I forgot your dad's a millionaire. You don't
act millionary any, naow. But a dory an' craft an' gear"—
Dan spoke as though she were a whaleboat—"costs a heap.
Think your dad 'u'd give you one fer—fer a pet like?"

"Should n't wonder. It would be 'most the only thing
I have n't stuck him for yet."

" 'Must be an expensive kinder kid to home. Don't
slitheroo thet way, Harve. Short 's the trick, because no
sea 's ever dead still, an' the swells 'll——"

Crack! The loom of the oar kicked Harvey under the
chin and knocked him backwards.

"That was what I was goin' to say. I hed to learn too,
but *I* was n't more than eight years old when I got my
schoolin'."

Harvey regained his seat with aching jaws and a frown.

"No good gettin' mad at things, Dad says. It 's our own
fault ef we can't handle 'em, he says. Le 's try here.
Manuel 'll give us the water."

The "Portugee" was rocking fully a mile away, but
when Dan up-ended an oar he waved his left arm three
times.

"Thirty fathom," said Dan, stringing a salt clam on to
the hook. "Over with the doughboys. Bait same 's I do,
Harvey, an' don't snarl your reel."

Dan's line was out long before Harvey had mastered the mystery of baiting and heaving out the leads. The dory drifted along easily. It was not worth while to anchor till they were sure of good ground.

"Here we come!" Dan shouted, and a shower of spray rattled on Harvey's shoulders as a big cod flapped and kicked alongside. "Muckle, Harvey, muckle! Under your hand! Quick!"

Evidently "muckle" could not be the dinner-horn, so Harvey passed over the maul, and Dan scientifically stunned the fish before he pulled it inboard, and wrenched out the hook with the short wooden stick he called a "gob-stick." Then Harvey felt a tug, and pulled up zealously. "Why, these are strawberries!" he shouted. "Look!"

The hook had fouled among a bunch of strawberries, red on one side and white on the other—perfect reproductions of the land fruit, except that there were no leaves, and the stem was all pipy and slimy.

"Don't tech 'em. Slat 'em off. Don't——"

The warning came too late. Harvey had picked them from the hook, and was admiring them.

"Ouch!" he cried, for his fingers throbbed as though he had grasped many nettles.

"Naow ye knows what strawberry-bottom means. Nothin' 'cep' fish should be teched with the naked fingers, Dad says. Slat 'em off agin the gunnel, an' bait up, Harve. Lookin' won't help any. It's all in the wages."

Harvey smiled at the thought of his ten and a half dollars a month, and wondered what his mother would say if she could see him hanging over the edge of a fishing-dory in mid-ocean. She suffered agonies whenever he went out on Saranac Lake; and, by the way, Harvey remembered distinctly that he used to laugh at her anxieties. Suddenly the line flashed through his hand, stinging even through the "nippers," the woolen circlets supposed to protect it.

"He's a logy. Give him room accordin' to his strength," cried Dan. "I'll help ye."

"No, you won't," Harvey snapped, as he hung on to the line. "It's my first fish. Is—is it a whale?"

"Halibut, mebbe." Dan peered down into the water alongside, and flourished the big "muckle," ready for all chances. Something white and oval flickered and fluttered through the green. "I 'll lay my wage an' share he 's over a hundred. Are you so everlastin' anxious to land him alone?"

Harvey's knuckles were raw and bleeding where they had been banged against the gunwale; his face was purple-blue between excitement and exertion; he dripped with sweat, and was half-blinded from staring at the circling sunlit ripples about the swiftly moving line. The boys were tired long ere the halibut, who took charge of them and the dory for the next twenty minutes. But the big flat fish was gaffed and hauled in at last.

"Beginner's luck," said Dan, wiping his forehead. "He 's all of a hundred."

Harvey looked at the huge gray-and-mottled creature with unspeakable pride. He had seen halibut many times on marble slabs ashore, but it had never occurred to him to ask how they came inland. Now he knew; and every inch of his body ached with fatigue.

"Ef Dad was along," said Dan, hauling up, "he 'd read the signs plain 's print. The fish are runnin' smaller an' smaller, an' you 've took 'baout as logy a halibut 's we 're apt to find this trip. Yesterday's catch—did ye notice it?—was all big fish an' no halibut. Dad he 'd read them signs right off. Dad says everythin' on the Banks is signs, an' can be read wrong er right. Dad's deeper 'n the Whale-hole."

Even as he spoke some one fired a pistol on the *We're Here,* and a potato-basket was run up in the fore-rigging.

"What did I say, naow? That 's the call fer the whole crowd. Dad 's onter something, er he 'd never break fishin' this time o' day. Reel up, Harve, and we 'll pull back."

They were to windward of the schooner, just ready to flirt the dory over the still sea, when sounds of woe half a mile off led them to Penn, who was careering around a fixed point for all the world like a gigantic water-bug. The little man backed away and came down again with enormous energy, but at the end of each manœuvre his dory swung round and snubbed herself on her rope.

"We 'll hev to help him, else he 'll root an' seed here," said Dan.

"What 's the matter?" said Harvey. This was a new world, where he could not lay down the law to his elders, but had

" 'I'll lay my wage an' share he's over a hundred.' "

to ask questions humbly. And the sea was horribly big and unexcited.

"Anchor 's fouled. Penn 's always losing 'em. Lost two this trip a'ready—on sandy bottom too—an' Dad says next one he loses, sure 's fishin', he 'll give him the kelleg. That 'u'd break Penn's heart."

"What 's a 'kelleg'?" said Harvey, who had a vague idea it might be some kind of marine torture, like keel-hauling in the story-books.

"Big stone instid of an anchor. You kin see a kelleg ridin' in the bows fur 's you can see a dory, an' all the Fleet knows what it means. They 'd guy him dreadful. Penn could n't stand that no more 'n a dog with a dipper to his tail. He's so everlastin' sensitive. Hello, Penn! Stuck again? Don't try any more o' your patents. Come up on her, and keep your rodin' straight up an' down."

"It does n't move," said the little man, panting. "It does n't move at all, and indeed I tried everything."

"What 's all this hurrah's-nest for'ard?" said Dan, pointing to a wild tangle of spare oars and dory-roding, all matted together by the hand of inexperience.

"Oh, that," said Penn proudly, "is a Spanish windlass. Mr. Salters showed me how to make it; but even *that* does n't move her."

Dan bent low over the gunwale to hide a smile, twitched once or twice on the roding, and, behold, the anchor drew at once.

"Haul up, Penn," he said laughing, "er she 'll git stuck again."

They left him regarding the weed-hung flukes of the little anchor with big, pathetic blue eyes, and thanking them profusely.

"Oh, say, while I think of it, Harve," said Dan when they were out of ear-shot, "Penn ain't quite all caulked. He ain't nowise dangerous, but his mind 's give out. See?"

"Is that so, or is it one of your father's judgments?" Harvey asked as he bent to his oars. He felt he was learning to handle them more easily.

"Dad ain't mistook this time. Penn 's a sure 'nuff loony. No, he ain't thet exactly, so much ez a harmless ijjit. It was this way (you 're rowin' quite so, Harve), an' I tell you 'cause it 's right you orter know. He was a Moravian preacher once. Jacob Boller wuz his name, Dad told me, an' he lived with his wife an' four children somewheres out Pennsylvania way. Well, Penn he took his folks along to a Moravian meetin'—camp-meetin' most like—an' they stayed over jest one night in Johnstown. You 've heered talk o' Johnstown?"

Harvey considered. "Yes, I have. But I don't know why. It sticks in my head same as Ashtabula."

"Both was big accidents—thet 's why, Harve. Well, that one single night Penn and his folks was to the hotel Johnstown was wiped out. 'Dam bust an' flooded her, an' the houses struck adrift an' bumped into each other an' sunk. I 've seen the pictures, an' they 're dretful. Penn he saw his folk drowned all 'n a heap 'fore he rightly knew what was comin'. His mind give out from that on. He mistrusted somethin' hed happened up to Johnstown, but for the poor life of him he could n't remember what, an' he jest drifted araound smilin' an' wonderin'. He did n't know what he was, nor yit what he hed bin, an' thet way he run agin Uncle Salters, who was visitin' 'n Allegheny City. Ha'af my mother's folks they live scattered inside o' Pennsylvania, an' Uncle Salters he visits araound winters. Uncle Salters he kinder adopted Penn, well knowin' what his trouble wuz; an' he brought him East, an' give him work on his farm."

"Why, I heard him calling Penn a farmer last night when the boats bumped. Is your Uncle Salters a farmer?"

"Farmer!" shouted Dan. "There ain't water enough 'tween here an' Hatt'rus to wash the furrer-mold off'n *his* boots. He 's jest everlastin' farmer. Why, Harve, I 've seen thet man hitch up a bucket, long towards sundown, an' set twiddlin' the spigot to the scuttle-butt same 's ef 't was a cow's bag. He's that much farmer. Well, Penn an' he they ran the farm—up Exeter way 't wuz. Uncle Salters he sold it this spring to a jay from Boston as wanted to build a summer-haouse, an' he got a heap for it. Well, them two loonies scratched along till, one day, Penn's church he 'd belonged to—the Moravians—found out where he wuz drifted an' layin', an' wrote to Uncle Salters. 'Never heerd what they said exactly; but Uncle Salters was mad. He 's a 'piscopolian mostly—but he jest let 'em hev it both sides o' the bow, 's if he was a Baptist; an' sez he war n't goin' to give up Penn to any blame Moravian connection in Pennsylvania or anywheres else. Then he come to Dad, towin' Penn,—thet was two trips back,—an' sez he an' Penn must fish a trip fer their health. 'Guess he thought the Moravians wouldn't hunt the Banks fer Jacob Boller. Dad was agreeable, fer Uncle Salters he 'd been fishin' off an' on fer thirty years, when he war n't inventin' patent manures, an' he took quarter-share in the *We 're Here;* an' the trip done Penn so much good, Dad made a habit o' takin' him. Some day, Dad sez, he 'll remember his wife an' kids *an'* Johnstown, an' then, like as not, he 'll die, Dad sez. Don't ye talk abaout Johnstown ner such things to Penn, 'r Uncle Salters he 'll heave ye overboard."

"Poor Penn!" murmured Harvey. "I should n't ever have thought Uncle Salters cared for him by the look of 'em together."

"I like Penn, though; we all do," said Dan. "We ought to ha' give him a tow, but I wanted to tell ye first."

They were close to the schooner now, the other boats a little behind them.

"You need n't heave in the dories till after dinner," said Troop from the deck. "We 'll dress daown right off. Fix table, boys!"

"Deeper 'n the Whale-deep," said Dan, with a wink, as he set the gear for dressing down. "Look at them boats that hev edged up sence mornin'. They're all waitin' on Dad. See 'em, Harve?"

"They are all alike to me." And indeed to a landsman, the nodding schooners around seemed run from the same mold.

"They ain't, though. That yaller, dirty packet with her bowsprit steeved that way, she 's the *Hope of Prague.* Nick Brady 's her skipper, the meanest man on the Banks. We 'll tell him so when we strike the Main Ledge. 'Way off yonder 's the *Day's Eye.* The two Jeraulds own her. She 's from Harwich; fastish, too, an' hez good luck; but Dad he 'd find fish in a graveyard. Them other three, side along, they 're the *Margie Smith, Rose,* and *Edith S. Walen,* all frum home. 'Guess we 'll see the *Abbie M. Deering* to-morrer, Dad, won't we? They 're all slippin' over from the shoal o' 'Queereau."

"You won't see many boats to-morrow, Danny." When

Troop called his son Danny, it was a sign that the old
man was pleased. "Boys, we 're too crowded," he went on,
addressing the crew as they clambered inboard. "We'll
leave 'em to bait big an' catch small." He looked at the
catch in the pen, and it was curious to see how little and
level the fish ran. Save for Harvey's halibut, there was
nothing over fifteen pounds on deck.

"I 'm waitin' on the weather," he added.

"Ye 'll have to make it yourself, Disko, for there 's no
sign I can see," said Long Jack, sweeping the clear horizon.

And yet, half an hour later, as they were dressing down,
the Bank fog dropped on them, "between fish and fish,"
as they say. It drove steadily and in wreaths, curling and
smoking along the colourless water. The men stopped
dressing-down without a word. Long Jack and Uncle Salters
slipped the windlass brakes into their sockets, and began to
heave up the anchor; the windlass jarring as the wet
hempen cable strained on the barrel. Manuel and Tom Platt
gave a hand at the last. The anchor came up with a sob,
and the riding-sail bellied as Troop steadied her at the
wheel. "Up jib and foresail," said he.

"Slip 'em in the smother," shouted Long Jack, making
fast the jib-sheet, while the others raised the clacking, rattling rings of the foresail; and the fore-boom creaked as
the *We 're Here* looked up into the wind and dived off
into blank, whirling white.

"There 's wind behind this fog," said Troop.

It was wonderful beyond words to Harvey; and the
most wonderful part was that he heard no orders except
an occasional grunt from Troop, ending with, "That's good,
my son!"

" 'Never seen anchor weighed before?" said Tom Platt,
to Harvey gaping at the damp canvas of the foresail.

"No. Where are we going?"

"Fish and make berth, as you 'll find out 'fore you 've
been a week aboard. It 's all new to you, but we never
know what may come to us. Now, take me—Tom Platt
—I'd never ha' thought——"

"It 's better than fourteen dollars a month an' a bullet
in your belly," said Troop, from the wheel. "Ease your
jumbo a grind."

"Dollars an' cents better," returned the man-o'-war's man, doing something to a big jib with a wooden spar tied to it. "But we did n't think 'o that when we manned the windlass-brakes on the *Miss Jim Buck*,[1] outside Beaufort Harbour, with Fort Macon heavin' hot shot at our stern, an' a livin' gale atop of all. Where was you then, Disko?"

"Jest here, or hereabouts," Disko replied, "earnin' my bread on the deep waters, an' dodgin' Reb privateers. Sorry I can't accommodate you with red-hot shot, Tom Platt; but I guess we 'll come aout all right on wind 'fore we see Eastern Point."

There was an incessant slapping and chatter at the bows now, varied by a solid thud and a little spout of spray that clattered down on the foc'sle. The rigging dripped clammy drops, and the men lounged along the lee of the house—all save Uncle Salters, who sat stiffly on the mainhatch nursing his stung hands.

" 'Guess she 'd carry stays'l," said Disko, rolling one eye at his brother.

" 'Guess she would n't to any sorter profit. What 's the sense o' wastin' canvas?" the farmer-sailor replied.

The wheel twitched almost imperceptibly in Disko's hands. A few seconds later a hissing wave-top slashed diagonally across the boat, smote Uncle Salters between the shoulders, and drenched him from head to foot. He rose sputtering, and went forward only to catch another.

"See Dad chase him all around the deck," said Dan. "Uncle Salters he thinks his quarter share 's our canvas. Dad 's put this duckin' act up on him two trips runnin'. Hi! That found him where he feeds." Uncle Salters had taken refuge by the foremast, but a wave slapped him over the knees. Disko's face was as blank as the circle of the wheel.

"Guess she 'd lie easier under stays'l, Salters," said Disko, as though he had seen nothing.

"Set your old kite, then," roared the victim through a cloud of spray; "only don't lay it to me if anything happens. Penn, you go below right off an' git your coffee. You ought to hev more sense than to bum araound on deck this weather."

[1] The *Gemsbok*, U.S.N.?

"Now they 'll swill coffee an' play checkers till the cows come home," said Dan, as Uncle Salters hustled Penn into the fore-cabin. " 'Looks to me like 's if we 'd all be doin' so fer a spell. There 's nothin' in creation deader-limpsey-idler 'n a Banker when she ain't on fish."

"I 'm glad ye spoke, Danny," cried Long Jack, who had been casting round in search of amusement. "I 'd clean forgot we 'd a passenger under that T-wharf hat. There 's no idleness for thim that don't know their ropes. Pass him along, Tom Platt, an' we 'll larn him."

" 'Tain't my trick this time," grinned Dan. "You 've got to go it alone. Dad learned *me* with a rope's end."

For an hour Long Jack walked his prey up and down, teaching, as he said, "things at the sea that ivry man must know, blind, dhrunk, or asleep." There is not much gear to a seventy-ton schooner with a stump-foremast, but Long Jack had a gift of expression. When he wished to draw Harvey's attention to the peak-halyards, he dug his knuckles into the back of the boy's neck and kept him at gaze for half a minute. He emphasized the difference between fore and aft generally by rubbing Harvey's nose along a few feet of the boom, and the lead of each rope was fixed in Harvey's mind by the end of the rope itself.

The lesson would have been easier had the deck been at all free; but there appeared to be a place on it for everything and anything except a man. Forward lay the windlass and its tackle, with the chain and hemp cables, all very unpleasant to trip over; the foc'sle stovepipe, and the gurry-butts by the foc'sle hatch to hold the fish-livers. Aft of these the fore-boom and booby of the main-hatch took all the space that was not needed for the pumps and dressing-pens. Then came the nests of dories lashed to ring-bolts by the quarter-deck; the house, with tubs and oddments lashed all around it; and, last, the sixty-foot main-boom in its crutch, splitting things lengthwise, to duck and dodge under every time.

Tom Platt, of course, could not keep his oar out of the business, but ranged alongside with enormous and unnecessary descriptions of sails and spars on the old *Ohio*.

"Niver mind fwhat he says; attind to me, Innocince. Tom Platt, this bally-hoo 's not the *Ohio*, an' you 're mixing the bhoy bad."

"He 'll be ruined for life, beginnin' on a fore-an'-after this way," Tom Platt pleaded. "Give him a chance to know a few leadin' principles. Sailin's an art, Harvey, as I 'd show you if I had ye in the fore-top o' the——"

"I know ut. Ye 'd talk him dead an' cowled. Silince, Tom Platt! Now, after all I 've said, how 'd you reef the foresail, Harve? Take your time answerin'."

"Haul that in," said Harvey, pointing to leeward.

"Fwhat? The North Atlantuc?"

"No, the boom. Then run that rope you showed me back there——"

"That 's no way," Tom Platt burst in.

"Quiet! He's larnin', an' has not the names good yet. Go on, Harve."

"Oh, it 's the reef-pennant. I'd hook the tackle on to the reef-pennant, and then let down——"

"Lower the sail, child! Lower!" said Tom Platt, in a professional agony.

"Lower the throat and peak halyards," Harvey went on. Those names stuck in his head.

"Lay your hand on thim," said Long Jack.

Harvey obeyed. "Lower till that rope-loop—on the after-leach—kris—no, it 's cringle—till the cringle was down on the boom. Then I 'd tie her up the way you said, and then I 'd hoist up the peak and throat halyards again."

"You 've forgot to pass the tack-earing, but wid time and help ye 'll larn. There 's good and just reason for ivry rope aboard, or else 't would be overboard. D 'ye follow me? 'T is dollars an' cents I'm puttin' into your pocket, ye skinny little supercargo, so that fwhin ye 've filled out ye can ship from Boston to Cuba an' tell thim Long Jack larned you. Now I 'll chase ye around a piece, callin' the ropes, an' you 'll lay your hand on thim as I call."

He began, and Harvey, who was feeling rather tired, walked slowly to the rope named. A rope's end licked round his ribs, and nearly knocked the breath out of him.

"When you own a boat," said Tom Platt, with severe eyes, "you can walk. Till then, take all orders at the run. Once more—to make sure!"

Harvey was in a glow with the exercise, and this last cut warmed him thoroughly. Now, he was a singularly smart boy, the son of a very clever man and a very sensitive woman, with a fine resolute temper that systematic spoiling had nearly turned to mulish obstinacy. He looked at the other men, and saw that even Dan did not smile. It was evidently all in the day's work, though it hurt abominably; so he swallowed the hint with a gulp and a gasp and a grin. The same smartness that led him to take such advantage of his mother made him very sure that no one on the boat, except, maybe, Penn, would stand the least nonsense. One learns a great deal from a mere tone. Long Jack called over half a dozen ropes, and Harvey danced over the deck like an eel at ebb-tide, one eye on Tom Platt.

"Ver' good. Ver' good don," said Manuel. "After supper I show you a little schooner I make, with all her ropes. So we shall learn."

"Fust-class fer—a passenger," said Dan. "Dad he 's jest allowed you 'll be wuth your salt maybe 'fore you 're draownded. Thet 's a heap fer Dad. I 'll learn you more our next watch together."

"Taller!" grunted Disko, peering through the fog as it smoked over the bows. There was nothing to be seen ten feet beyond the surging jib-boom, while alongside rolled the endless procession of solemn, pale waves whispering and lipping one to the other.

"Now I 'll learn you something Long Jack can't," shouted Tom Platt, as from a locker by the stern he produced a battered deep-sea lead hollowed at one end, smeared the hollow from a saucer full of mutton tallow, and went forward. "I 'll learn you how to fly the Blue Pigeon. Shooo!"

Disko did something to the wheel that checked the schooner's way, while Manuel, with Harvey to help (and a proud boy was Harvey), let down the jib in a lump on the boom. The lead sung a deep droning song as Tom Platt whirled it round and round.

"Go ahead, man," said Long Jack, impatiently. "We 're not drawin' twenty-five fut off Fire Island in a fog. There 's no trick to ut."

"Don't be jealous, Galway." The released lead plopped into the sea far ahead as the schooner surged slowly forward.

"Soundin' *is* a trick, though," said Dan, "when your dipsey lead 's all the eye you 're like to hev for a week. What d' you make it, Dad?"

Disko's face relaxed. His skill and honour were involved in the march he had stolen on the rest of the Fleet, and he had his reputation as a master artist who knew the Banks blindfold. "Sixty, mebbe—ef I'm any judge," he replied, with a glance at the tiny compass in the window of the house.

"Sixty," sung out Tom Platt, hauling in great wet coils.

The schooner gathered way once more, "Heave!" said Disko, after a quarter of an hour.

"What d' you make it?" Dan whispered, and he looked at Harvey proudly. But Harvey was too proud of his own performances to be impressed just then.

"Fifty," said the father. "I mistrust we 're right over the nick o' Green Bank on old Sixty-Fifty."

"Fifty!" roared Tom Platt. They could scarcely see him through the fog. "She 's bust within a yard—like the shells at Fort Maçon."

"Bait up, Harve," said Dan, diving for a line on the reel.

The schooner seemed to be straying promiscuously through the smother, her headsail banging wildly. The men waited and looked at the boys who began fishing.

"Heugh!" Dan's lines twitched on the scored and scarred rail. "Now haow in thunder did Dad know? Help us here, Harve. It 's a big un. Poke-hooked, too." They hauled together, and landed a goggle-eyed twenty-pound cod. He had taken the bait right into his stomach.

"Why, he 's all covered with little crabs," cried Harvey, turning him over.

"By the great hook-block, they 're lousy already," said Long Jack. "Disko, ye kape your spare eyes under the keel."

Splash went the anchor, and they all heaved over the lines, each man taking his own place at the bulwarks.

"Are they good to eat?" Harvey panted, as he lugged in another crab-covered cod.

"Sure. When they 're lousy it 's a sign they 've all been herdin' together by the thousand, and when they take the bait that way they 're hungry. Never mind how the bait sets. They 'll bite on the bare hook."

"Say, this is great!" Harvey cried, as the fish came in gasping and splashing—nearly all poke-hooked, as Dan had said. "Why can't we always fish from the boat instead of from the dories?"

"Allus can, till we begin to dress daown. Efter thet, the heads and offals 'u'd scare the fish to Fundy. Boat-fishin' ain't reckoned progressive, though, unless you know as much as dad knows. Guess we 'll run aout aour trawl to-night. Harder on the back, this, than frum the dory, ain't it?"

It was rather back-breaking work, for in a dory the weight of a cod is water-borne till the last minute, and you are, so to speak, abreast of him; but the few feet of a schooner's freeboard make so much extra dead-hauling, and stooping over the bulwarks cramps the stomach. But it was wild and furious sport so long as it lasted; and a big pile lay aboard when the fish ceased biting.

"Where 's Penn and Uncle Salters?" Harvey asked, slapping the slime off his oilskins, and reeling up the line in careful imitation of the others.

"Git 's coffee and see."

Under the yellow glare of the lamp on the pawl-post, the foc'sle table down and opened, utterly unconscious of fish or weather, sat the two men, a checker-board between them, Uncle Salters snarling at Penn's every move.

"What 's the matter naow?" said the former, as Harvey, one hand in the leather loop at the head of the ladder, hung shouting to the cook.

"Big fish and lousy—heaps and heaps," Harvey replied, quoting Long Jack. "How 's the game?"

Little Penn's jaw dropped. "'T were n't none o' his fault," snapped Uncle Salters. "Penn 's deef."

"Checkers, were n't it?" said Dan, as Harvey staggered aft with the steaming coffee in a tin pail. "That lets us out o' cleanin' up to-night. Dad 's a jest man. They 'll have to do it."

"An' two young fellers I know 'll bait up a tub or so o' trawl, while they 're cleanin'," said Disko, lashing the wheel to his taste.

"Um! Guess I 'd ruther clean up, Dad."

"Don't doubt it. Ye wun't, though. Dress daown! Dress daown! Penn 'll pitch while you two bait up."

"Why in thunder did n't them blame boys tell us you 'd struck on?" said Uncle Salters, shuffling to his place at the table. "This knife 's gum-blunt, Dan."

"Ef stickin' out cable don't wake ye, guess you 'd better hire a boy o' your own," said Dan, muddling about in the dusk over the tubs full of trawl-line lashed to windward of the house. "Oh, Harve, don't ye want to slip down an' git 's bait?"

"Bait ez we are," said Disko. "I mistrust shag-fishin' will pay better, ez things go."

That meant the boys would bait with selected offal of the cod as the fish were cleaned—an improvement on paddling bare-handed in the little bait-barrels below. The tubs were full of neatly coiled line carrying a big hook each few feet; and the testing and baiting of every single hook, with the stowage of the baited line so that it should run clear when shot from the dory, was a scientific business. Dan managed it in the dark, without looking, while Harvey caught his fingers on the barbs and bewailed his fate. But the hooks flew through Dan's fingers like tatting on an old maid's lap. "I helped bait up trawl ashore 'fore I could well walk," he said. "But it 's a putterin' job all the same. Oh, Dad!" This shouted towards the hatch, where Disko and Tom Platt were salting. "How many skates you reckon we 'll need?"

" 'Baout three. Hurry!"

"There's three hundred fathom to each tub," Dan explained; "more 'n enough to lay out to-night. Ouch! 'Slipped up there, I did." He stuck his finger in his mouth. "I tell you, Harve, there ain't money in Gloucester 'u'd hire me to ship on a reg'lar trawler. It may be progressive, but, barrin' that, it 's the putterin'est, slimjammest business top of earth."

"I don't know what this is, if 't is n't regular trawling," said Harvey sulkily. "My fingers are all cut to frazzles."

"Pshaw! This is just one o' Dad's blame experiments. He don't trawl 'less there 's mighty good reason fer it. Dad knows. Thet 's why he 's baitin' ez he is. We 'll hev her saggin' full when we take her up er we won't see a fin."

Penn and Uncle Salters cleaned up as Disko had ordained, but the boys profited little. No sooner were the tubs furnished than Tom Platt and Long Jack, who had been exploring the inside of a dory with a lantern, snatched them away, loaded up the tubs and some small, painted trawl-buoys, and hove the boat overboard into what Harvey regarded as an exceedingly rough sea. "They'll be drowned. Why, the dory's loaded like a freight-car," he cried.

"We 'll be back," said Long Jack, "an' in case you 'll not be lookin' for us, we 'll lay into you both if the trawl's snarled."

The dory surged up on the crest of a wave, and just when it seemed impossible that she could avoid smashing against the schooner's side, slid over the ridge, and was swallowed up in the damp dusk.

"Take ahold here, an' keep ringin' steady," said Dan, passing Harvey the lanyard of a bell that hung just behind the windlass.

Harvey rang lustily, for he felt two lives depended on him. But Disko in the cabin, scrawling in the log-book, did not look like a murderer, and when he went to supper he even smiled dryly at the anxious Harvey.

"*This* ain't no weather," said Dan. "Why, you an' me could set thet trawl! They 've only gone out jest far 'nough so 's not to foul our cable. They don't need no bell reely."

"Clang! clang! clang!" Harvey kept it up, varied with occasional rub-a-dubs, for another half-hour. There was a bellow and a bump alongside. Manuel and Dan raced to the hooks of the dory-tackle; Long Jack and Tom Platt arrived on deck together, it seemed, one half the North Atlantic at their backs, and the dory followed them in the air, landing with a clatter.

"Nary snarl," said Tom Platt as he dripped. "Danny, you 'll do yet."

"The pleasure av your comp'ny to the banquit," said Long Jack, squelching the water from his boots as he capered like an elephant and stuck an oil-skinned arm into Harvey's face. "We do be condescending to honour the second half wid our presence." And off they all four rolled to supper, where Harvey stuffed himself to the brim on fish-chowder and fried pies, and fell fast asleep just as Manuel produced from a locker a lovely two-foot model of the *Lucy Holmes,* his first boat, and was going to show Harvey the ropes. Harvey never even twiddled his fingers as Penn pushed him into his bunk.

"It must be a sad thing—a very sad thing," said Penn,

watching the boy's face, "for his mother and his father, who think he is dead. To lose a child—to lose a manchild!"

"Git out o' this, Penn," said Dan. "Go aft and finish your game with Uncle Salters. Tell Dad I 'll stand Harve's watch ef he don't keer. He 's played aout."

"Ver' good boy," said Manuel, slipping out of his boots and disappearing into the black shadows of the lower bunk. "Expec' he make good man, Danny. I no see he is any so mad as your parpa he says. Eh, wha-at?"

Dan chuckled, but the chuckle ended in a snore.

It was thick weather outside, with a rising wind, and the elder men stretched their watches. The hour struck clear in the cabin; the nosing bows slapped and scuffed with the seas; the foc'sle stove-pipe hissed and sputtered as the spray caught it; and the boys slept on, while Disko, Long Jack, Tom Platt, and Uncle Salters, each in turn, stumped aft to look at the wheel, forward to see that the anchor held, or to veer out a little more cable against chafing, with a glance at the dim anchor-light between each round.

# CHAPTER IV

HARVEY WAKED to find the "first half" at breakfast, the foc'sle door drawn to a crack, and every square inch of the schooner singing its own tune. The black bulk of the cook balanced behind the tiny galley over the glare of the stove, and the pots and pans in the pierced wooden board before it jarred and racketed to each plunge. Up and up the foc'sle climbed, yearning and surging and quivering, and then, with a clear, sickle-like swoop, came down into the seas. He could hear the flaring bows cut and squelch, and there was a pause ere the divided waters came down on the deck above, like a volley of buckshot. Followed the woolly sound of the cable in the hawsehole; and a grunt and squeal of the windlass; a yaw, a punt, and a kick, and the *We 're Here* gathered herself together to repeat the motions.

"Now, ashore," he heard Long Jack saying, "ye 've chores, an' ye must do thim in any weather. Here we 're well clear of the fleet, an' we 've no chores—an' that 's a blessin'. Good night, all." He passed like a big snake from the table to his bunk, and began to smoke. Tom Platt followed his example; Uncle Salters, with Penn, fought his way up the ladder to stand his watch, and the cook set for the "second half."

It came out of its bunks as the others had entered theirs, with a shake and a yawn. It ate till it could eat no more; and then Manuel filled his pipe with some terrible tobacco, crotched himself between the pawl-post and a forward bunk, cocked his feet up on the table, and smiled tender and indolent smiles at the smoke. Dan lay at length in his bunk, wrestling with a gaudy, gilt-stopped accordion, whose tunes went up and down with the pitching of the *We 're Here*. The cook, his shoulders against the locker where he kept the fried pies (Dan was fond of fried pies), peeled potatoes, with one eye on the stove in event of too much

water finding its way down the pipe; and the general smell
and smother were past all description.

Harvey considered affairs, wondered that he was not
deathly sick, and crawled into his bunk again, as the softest
and safest place, while Dan struck up, "I don't want to
play in your yard," as accurately as the wild jerks allowed.

"How long is this for?" Harvey asked of Manuel.

"Till she get a little quiet, and we can row to trawl.
Perhaps to-night. Perhaps two days more. You do not like?
Eh, wha-at?"

"I should have been crazy sick a week ago, but it does n't
seem to upset me now—much."

"That is because we make you fisherman, these days. If
I was you, when I come to Gloucester I would give two,
three big candles for my good luck."

"Give who?"

"To be sure—the Virgin of our Church on the Hill. She
is very good to fishermen all the time. That is why so few
of us Portugee men ever are drowned."

"You're a Roman Catholic, then?"

"I am a Madeira man. I am not a Porto Pico boy. Shall
I be Baptist, then? Eh, what-at? I always give candles—
two, three more when I come to Gloucester. The good
Virgin she never forgets me, Manuel."

"I don't sense it that way," Tom Platt put in from his
bunk, his scarred face lit up by the glare of a match as he
sucked at his pipe. "It stands to reason the sea's the sea;
and you 'll get jest about what 's goin', candles or kerosene,
fer that matter."

" 'T is a mighty good thing," said Long Jack, "to have
a frind at coort, though. I'm o' Manuel's way o' thinkin'.
About tin years back I was crew to a Sou' Boston market-
boat. We was off Minot's Ledge wid a northeaster, butt
first, atop of us, thicker 'n burgoo. The ould man was
dhrunk, his chin waggin' on the tiller, an' I sez to myself,
'If iver I stick my boat-huk into T-wharf again, I 'll show
the saints fwhat manner o' craft they saved me out av.'
Now, I 'm here, as ye can well see, an' the model of the
dhirty ould *Kathleen*, that took me a month to make, I
gave ut to the priest, an' he hung ut up forninst the altar.
There 's more sense in givin' a model that 's by way o'
bein' a work av art than any candle. Ye can buy candles at

store, but a model shows the good saints ye 've tuk trouble
an' are grateful."

"D' you believe that, Irish?" said Tom Platt, turning on
his elbow.

"Would I do ut if I did not, Ohio?"

"Wa-al, Enoch Fuller he made a model o' the old *Ohio*,
and she 's to Calem museum now. Mighty pretty model,
too, but I guess Enoch he never done it fer no sacrifice;
an' the way I take it is——"

There were the makings of an hour-long discussion of
the kind that fishermen love, where the talk runs in shouting circles and no one proves anything at the end, had not
Dan struck up this cheerful rhyme:

> "Up jumped the mackerel with his stripèd back.
> Reef in the mainsail, and haul on the tack;
> *For* it's windy weather——"

Here Long Jack joined in:

> *"And* it's blowy weather;
> *When* the winds begin to blow, pipe all hands together!"

Dan went on, with a cautious look at Tom Platt, holding the accordion low in the bunk:

> "Up jumped the cod with his chuckle-head,
> Went to the main-chains to heave at the lead;
> *For* it's windy weather," etc.

Tom Platt seemed to be hunting for something. Dan
crouched lower, but sang louder:

> "Up jumped the flounder that swims to the ground.
> Chuckle-head! Chuckle-head! Mind where ye sound!"

Tom Platt's huge rubber boot whirled across the foc'sle
and caught Dan's uplifted arm. There was war between
the man and the boy ever since Dan had discovered that
the mere whistling of that tune would make him angry as
he heaved the lead.

"Thought I 'd fetch yer," said Dan, returning the gift
with precision. "Ef you don't like my music, git out your
fiddle. I ain't goin' to lie here all day an' listen to you an'

Long Jack arguin' 'baout candles. Fiddle, Tom Platt; or I 'll learn Harve here the tune!"

Tom Platt leaned down to a locker and brought up an old white fiddle. Manuel's eye glistened, and from somewhere behind the pawl-post he drew out a tiny, guitar-like thing with wire strings, which he called a *machette*.

" 'T is a concert," said Long Jack, beaming through the smoke. "A reg'lar Boston concert."

There was a burst of spray as the hatch opened, and Disko, in yellow oilskins, descended.

"Ye 're just in time, Disko. Fwhat 's she doin' outside?"

"Jest this!" He dropped on to the lockers with the push and heave of the *We 're Here*.

"We 're singin' to kape our breakfasts down. Ye 'll lead, av course, Disko," said Long Jack.

"Guess there ain't more 'n 'baout two old songs I know, an' ye 've heerd them both."

His excuses were cut short by Tom Platt launching into a most dolorous tune, like unto the moaning of winds and the creaking of masts. With his eyes fixed on the beams above, Disko began this ancient, ancient ditty, Tom Platt flourishing all round him to make the tune and words fit a little:

"There is a crack packet—crack packet o' fame,
She hails from Noo York, an' the *Dreadnought*'s her name.
You may talk o' your fliers—Swallow-tail and Black Ball—
But the *Dreadnought*'s the packet that can beat them all.

"Now the *Dreadnought* she lies in the River Mersey,
Because of the tug-boat to take her to sea;
But when she's off soundings you shortly will know

(*Chorus.*)
She's the Liverpool packet—O Lord, let her go!

"Now the *Dreadnought* she's howlin' crost the Banks o' Newfoundland,
Where the water's all shallow and the bottom's all sand.
Sez all the little fishes that swim to and fro:

(*Chorus.*)
'She's the Liverpool packet—O Lord, let her go!' "

There were scores of verses, for he worked the *Dread-*

*nought* every mile of the way between Liverpool and New York as conscientiously as though he were on her deck, and the accordion pumped and the fiddle squeaked beside him. Tom Platt followed with something about "the rough and tough McGinn, who would pilot the vessel in." Then they called on Harvey, who felt very flattered, to contribute to the entertainment; but all that he could remember were some pieces of "Skipper Ireson's Ride" that he had been taught at the camp-school in the Adirondacks. It seemed that they might be appropriate to the time and place, but he had no more than mentioned the title when Disko brought down one foot with a bang, and cried, "Don't go on, young feller. That's a mistaken jedgment—one o' the worst kind, too, becaze it 's catchin' to the ear."

"I orter ha' warned you," said Dan. "Thet allus fetches Dad."

"What 's wrong?" said Harvey, surprised and a little angry.

"All you 're goin' to say," said Disko. "All dead wrong from start to finish, an' Whittier he 's to blame. I have no special call to right any Marblehead man, but 't were n't no fault o' Ireson's. My father he told me the tale time an' again, an' this is the way 't wuz."

"For the wan hundredth time," put in Long Jack under his breath.

"Ben Ireson he was skipper o' the *Betty,* young feller, comin' home frum the Banks—that was before the war of 1812, but jestice is jestice at all times. They f'und the *Active* o' Portland, an' Gibbons o' that town he was her skipper; they f'und her leakin' off Cape Cod Light. There was a terr'ble gale on, an' they was gettin' the *Betty* home 's fast as they could craowd her. Well, Ireson he said there war n't any sense to reskin' a boat in that sea; the men they would n't hev it; and he laid it before them to stay by the *Active* till the sea run daown a piece. They would n't hev that either, hangin' araound the Cape in any sech weather, leak or no leak. They jest up stays'l and quit, nat'rally takin' Ireson with 'em. Folks to Marblehead was mad at him not runnin' the risk, and becaze nex' day, when the sea was ca'am (they never stopped to think o' *that*), some of the *Active's* folks was took off by a Truro man. They come into Marblehead with their own tale to tell, sayin' how Ireson had shamed his town, an' so forth an' so on; an' Ireson's men they was scared, seein' public feelin' agin' 'em, an' they went back on Ireson, an' swore he was respons'ble for the hull act. 'T were n't the women neither that tarred and feathered him—Marblehead women don't act that way—'t was a passel o' men an' boys, an' they carted him araound town in an old dory till the bottom fell aout, and Ireson he told 'em they 'd be sorry for it some day. Well, the facts come aout later, same 's they usually do, too late to be any ways useful to an honest man; an' Whittier he come along an' picked up the slack eend of a lyin' tale, an' tarred and feathered Ben Ireson all over onct more after he was dead. 'T was the only time Whittier ever slipped up, an' 't were n't fair. I whaled Dan good when he brought that piece back from school. *You* don't know no better, o' course; but I 've give you the facts, hereafter an' evermore to be remembered. Ben Ireson were n't no sech kind o' man as Whittier makes aout; my father he knew him well, before an' after that business, an' you beware o' hasty jedgments, young feller. Next!"

Harvey had never heard Disko talk so long, and collapsed with burning cheeks; but, as Dan said promptly, a boy could only learn what he was taught at school, and life was too short to keep track of every lie along the coast.

Then Manuel touched the jangling, jarring little *machette* to a queer tune, and sang something in Portuguese about *"Nina, innocente!"* ending with a full-handed sweep that brought the song up with a jerk. Then Disko obliged with his second song, to an old-fashioned creaky tune, and all joined in the chorus. This is one stanza:

"Now Aprile is over and melted the snow,
And outer Noo Bedford we shortly must tow;
Yes, out o' Noo Bedford we shortly must clear,
We're the whalers that never see wheat in the ear."

Here the fiddle went very softly for a while by itself, and then:

"Wheat-in-the-ear, my true-love's posy blowin';
Wheat-in-the-ear, we're goin' off to sea;
Wheat-in-the-ear, I left you fit for sowin';
When I come back a loaf o' bread you'll be!"

That made Harvey almost weep, though he could not
tell why. But it was much worse when the cook dropped
the potatoes and held out his hands for the fiddle. Still
leaning against the locker door, he struck into a tune that
was like something very bad but sure to happen whatever
you did. After a little he sang, in an unknown tongue,
his big chin down on the fiddle-tail, his white eyeballs
glaring in the lamp-light. Harvey swung out of his bunk
to hear better; and amid the straining of the timbers and
the wash of the waters the tune crooned and moaned
on, like lee surf in a blind fog, till it ended with a wail.

"Jiminy Christmas! Thet gives me the blue creevles,"
said Dan. "What in thunder is it?"

"The song of Fin McCoul," said the cook, "when he
wass going to Norway." His English was not thick, but
all clear-cut, as though it came from a phonograph.

"Faith, I've been to Norway, but I did n't make that
unwholesim noise. 'T is like some of the old songs, though,"
said Long Jack, sighing.

"Don't let 's hev another 'thout somethin' between,"
said Dan; and the accordion struck up a rattling, catchy
tune that ended:

"It's six an' twenty Sundays sence las' we saw the land,
        With fifteen hunder quintal,
        An' fifteen hunder quintal,
        'Teen hunder toppin' quintal,
        'Twix' old 'Queereau an' Grand!"

"Hold on!" roared Tom Platt. "D' ye want to nail the
trip, Dan? That 's Jonah sure, 'less you sing it after all
our salt 's wet."

"No, 't ain't. Is it Dad? Not unless you sing the very
las' verse. You can't learn *me* anything on Jonahs!"

"What 's that?" said Harvey. "What 's a Jonah?"

"A Jonah 's anything that spoils the luck. Sometimes
it 's a man—sometimes it 's a boy—or a bucket. I 've
known a splittin'-knife Jonah two trips till we was on to

her," said Tom Platt. "There's all sorts o' Jonahs. Jim Bourke was one till he was drowned on Georges. I'd never ship with Jim Bourke, not if I was starvin'. There wuz a green dory on the *Ezra Flood*. Thet was a Jonah, too, the worst sort o' Jonah. Drowned four men, she did, an' used to shine fiery o' nights in the nest."

"And you believe that?" said Harvey, remembering what Tom Platt had said about candles and models. "Have n't we all got to take what 's served?"

A mutter of dissent ran round the bunks. "Outboard, yes; inboard, things can happen," said Disko. "Don't you go makin' a mock of Jonahs, young feller."

"Well, Harve ain't no Jonah. Day after we catched him," Dan cut in, "we had a toppin' good catch."

The cook threw up his head and laughed suddenly— a queer, thin laugh. He was a most disconcerting man.

"Murder!" said Long Jack. "Don't do that again, doctor. We ain't used to ut."

"What 's wrong?" said Dan. "Ain't he our mascot, and did n't they strike on good after we 'd struck him?"

"Oh! yess," said the cook. "I know that, but the catch iss not finish yet."

"He ain't goin' to do us any harm," said Dan, hotly. "Where are ye hintin' an' edgin' to? *He 's* all right."

"No harm. No. But one day he will be your master, Danny."

"That all?" said Dan, placidly. "He wun't—not by a jugful."

"Master!" said the cook, pointing to Harvey. "Man!" and he pointed to Dan.

"That 's news. Haow soon?" said Dan, with a laugh.

"In some years, and I shall see it. Master and man— man and master."

"How in thunder d' ye work that out?" said Tom Platt.

"In my head, where I can see."

"Haow?" This from all the others at once.

"I do not know, but so it will be." He dropped his head, and went on peeling the potatoes, and not another word could they get out of him.

"Well," said Dan, "a heap o' things 'll hev to come abaout 'fore Harve 's any master o' mine; but I 'm glad

the doctor ain't choosen to mark him for a Jonah. Now,
I mistrust Uncle Salters fer the Jonerest Jonah in the
Fleet regardin' his own special luck. Dunno ef it 's
spreadin' same 's smallpox. He ought to be on the *Carrie
Pitman.* That boat 's her own Jonah, sure—crews an' gear
made no differ to her driftin'. Jiminy Christmas! She 'll
etch loose in a flat ca'am."

"We 're well clear o' the Fleet, anyway," said Disko.
*"Carrie Pitman* an' all." There was a rapping on the deck.

"Uncle Salters has catched his luck," said Dan as his
father departed.

"It 's blown clear," Disko cried, and all the foc'sle
tumbled up for a bit of fresh air. The fog had gone, but
a sullen sea ran in great rollers behind it. The *We 're
Here* slid, as it were, into long, sunk avenues and ditches
which felt quite sheltered and homelike if they would
only stay still; but they changed without rest or mercy,
and flung up the schooner to crown one peak of a thousand gray hills, while the wind hooted through her rigging
as she zigzagged down the slopes. Far away a sea would
burst into a sheet of foam, and the others would follow
suit as at a signal, till Harvey's eyes swam with the vision
of interlacing whites and grays. Four or five Mother
Carey's chickens stormed round in circles, shrieking as
they swept past the bows. A rain-squall or two strayed
aimlessly over the hopeless waste, ran down wind and
back again, and melted away.

"Seems to me I saw somethin' flicker jest naow over
yonder," said Uncle Salters, pointing to the northeast.

"Can't be any of the fleet," said Disko, peering under
his eyebrows, a hand on the foc'sle gangway as the solid
bows hatcheted into the troughs. "Sea's oilin' over dretful
fast. Danny, don't you want to skip up a piece an' see
how aour trawl-buoy lays?"

Danny, in his big boots, trotted rather than climbed
up the main rigging (this consumed Harvey with envy),
hitched himself around the reeling cross-trees, and let his
eye rove till it caught the tiny black buoy-flag on the
shoulder of a mile-away swell.

"She 's all right," he hailed. "Sail O! Dead to the
no'th'ard, comin' down like smoke! Schooner she be, too."

They waited yet another half-hour, the sky clearing in

patches, with a flicker of sickly sun from time to time that made patches of olive-green water. Then a stump-foremast lifted, ducked, and disappeared, to be followed on the next wave by a high stern with old-fashioned wooden snail's-horn davits. The sails were red-tanned.

"Frenchmen!" shouted Dan. "No, 't ain't, neither. Da-ad!"

"That 's no French," said Disko. "Salters, your blame luck holds tighter 'n a screw in a keg-head."

"I 've eyes. It 's Uncle Abishai."

"You can't nowise tell fer sure."

"The head-king of all Jonahs," groaned Tom Platt. "Oh, Salters, Salters, why was n't you abed an' asleep?"

"How could I tell?" said poor Salters, as the schooner swung up.

She might have been the very *Flying Dutchman,* so foul, draggled, and unkempt was every rope and stick aboard. Her old-style quarterdeck was some four or five feet high, and her rigging flew knotted and tangled like weed at a wharf-end. She was running before the wind—yawing frightfully—her staysail let down to act as a sort of extra foresail,—"scandalized," they call it,—and her foreboom guyed out over the side. Her bowsprit cocked up like an old-fashioned frigate's; her jib-boom had been fished and spliced and nailed and clamped beyond further repair; and as she hove herself forward, and sat down on her broad tail, she looked for all the world like a blouzy, frouzy, bad old woman sneering at a decent girl.

"That 's Abishai," said Salters. "Full o' gin an' Judique men, an' the judgments o' Providence layin' fer him an' never takin' good holt. He 's run in to bait, Miquelon way."

"He 'll run her under," said Long Jack. "That 's no rig fer this weather."

"Not he, 'r he 'd 'a' done it long ago," Disko replied. "Looks 's if he cal'lated to run *us* under. Ain't she daown by the head more 'n natural, Tom Platt?"

"Ef it 's his style o' loadin' her she ain't safe," said the sailor slowly. "Ef she 's spewed her oakum he 'd better git to his pumps mighty quick."

The creature threshed up, wore round with a clatter and rattle, and lay head to wind within ear-shot.

A gray-beard wagged over the bulwark, and a thick

voice yelled something Harvey could not understand. But Disko's face darkened. "He 'd resk every stick he hez to carry bad news. Says we 're in fer a shift o' wind. He 's in fer worse. Abishai! Abi-*shi!*" He waved his arm up and down with the gesture of a man at the pumps, and pointed forward. The crew mocked him and laughed.

"Jounce ye, an' strip ye an' trip ye!" yelled Uncle Abishai. "A livin' gale—a livin' gale. Yah! Cast up fer your last trip, all you Gloucester haddocks. *You* won't see Gloucester no more, no more!"

"Crazy full—as usual," said Tom Platt. "Wish he had n't spied us, though."

She drifted out of hearing while the gray-head yelled something about a dance at the Bay of Bulls and a dead man in the foc'sle. Harvey shuddered. He had seen the sloven tilled decks and the savage-eyed crew.

"An' that 's a fine little floatin' hell fer her draught," said Long Jack. "I wondher what mischief he 's been at ashore."

"He 's a trawler," Dan explained to Harvey, "an' he runs in fer bait all along the coast. Oh, no, not home, he don't go. He deals along the south an' east shore up yonder." He nodded in the direction of the pitiless Newfoundland beaches. "Dad won't never take me ashore there. They 're a mighty tough crowd—an' Abishai 's the toughest. You saw his boat? Well, she 's nigh seventy year old, they say; the last o' the old Marblehead heeltappers. They don't make them quarterdecks any more. Abishai don't use Marblehead, though. He ain't wanted there. He jes' drif's araound, in debt, trawlin' an' cussin' like you 've heard. Bin a Jonah fer years an' years, he hez. 'Gits liquor frum the Feecamp boats fer makin' spells an' selling winds an' such truck. Crazy, I guess."

" 'T won't be any use underrunnin' the trawl to-night," said Tom Platt, with quiet despair. "He come alongside special to cuss us. I 'd give my wage an' share to see him at the gangway o' the old *Ohio* 'fore we quit floggin'. Jest abaout six dozen, an' Sam Mocatta layin' 'em on crisscross!"

The dishevelled "heel-tapper" danced drunkenly down wind, and all eyes followed her. Suddenly the cook cried in his phonograph voice: "It wass his own death made him speak so! He iss fey—fey, I tell you! Look!" She sailed into a patch of watery sunshine three or four miles distant. The patch dulled and faded out, and even as the light passed so did the schooner. She dropped into a hollow and—was not.

"Run under, by the Great Hook-Block!" shouted Disko, jumping aft. "Drunk or sober, we 've got to help 'em. Heave short and break her out! Smart!"

Harvey was thrown on the deck by the shock that followed the setting of the jib and foresail, for they hove short on the cable, and to save time, jerked the anchor bodily from the bottom, heaving in as they moved away. This is a bit of brute force seldom resorted to except in matters of life and death, and the little *We 're Here* complained like a human. They ran down to where Abishai 's craft had vanished; found two or three trawl-tubs, a gin-botttle, and a stove-in dory, but nothing more. "Let 'em go," said Disko, though no one had hinted at picking them up. "I would n't hev a match that belonged to Abishai aboard. Guess she run clear under. Must ha' been spewin' her oakum fer a week, an' they never thought to pump her. That 's one more boat gone along o' leavin' port all hands drunk."

"Glory be!" said Long Jack. "We 'd ha' been obliged to help 'em if they was top o' water."

" 'Thinkin' o' that myself," said Tom Platt.

"Fey! Fey!" said the cook, rolling his eyes. "He haas taken his own luck with him."

"Ver' good thing, I think, to tell the Fleet when we see. Eh, wha-at?" said Manuel. "If you runna that way before the wind, and she work open her seams——" He threw out his hands with an indescribable gesture, while Penn sat down on the house and sobbed at the sheer horror and pity of it all. Harvey could not realize that he had seen death on the open waters, but he felt very sick.

Then Dan went up the cross-trees, and Disko steered them back to within sight of their own trawl-buoys just before the fog blanketed the sea once again.

"We go mighty quick hereabouts when we do go," was all he said to Harvey. "You think on that fer a spell, young feller. That was liquor."

After dinner it was calm enough to fish from the decks,

—Penn and Uncle Salters were very zealous this time,—
and the catch was large and large fish.

"Abishai has shorely took his luck with him," said
Salters. "The wind hain't backed ner riz ner nothin'.
How abaout the trawl? I despise superstition, anyway."

Tom Platt insisted that they had much better haul the
thing and make a new berth. But the cook said: "The
luck iss in two pieces. You will find it so when you look.
I know." This so tickled Long Jack that he overbore Tom
Platt and the two went out together.

Underrunning a trawl means pulling it in on one side
of the dory, picking off the fish, rebaiting the hooks, and
passing them back to the sea again—something like pin-
ning and unpinning linen on a wash-line. It is a lengthy
business and rather dangerous, for the long, sagging line
may twitch a boat under in a flash. But when they heard,
"And naow to thee, O Capting," booming out of the fog,
the crew of the We 're Here took heart. The dory swirled
alongside well loaded, Tom Platt yelling for Manuel to
act as relief-boat.

"The luck 's cut square in two pieces," said Long Jack,
forking in the fish, while Harvey stood open-mouthed
at the skill with which the plunging dory was saved from
destruction. "One half was jest punkins. Tom Platt wanted
to haul her an' ha' done wid ut; but I said, 'I 'll back the
doctor that has the second sight,' an' the other half come
up sagging full o' big uns. Hurry, Man'nle, an' bring 's a
tub o' bait. There 's luck afloat to-night."

The fish bit at the newly baited hooks from which their
brethren had just been taken, and Tom Platt and Long
Jack moved methodically up and down the length of the
trawl, the boat's nose surging under the wet line of hooks,
stripping the sea-cucumbers that they called pumpkins,
slatting off the fresh-caught cod against the gunwale, rebaiting, and loading Manuel's dory till dusk.

"I 'll take no risks," said Disko then—"not with him
floatin' around so near. Abishai won't sink fer a week.
Heave in the dories an' we 'll dress daown after supper."

That was a mighty dressing-down, attended by three
or four blowing grampuses. It lasted till nine o'clock, and
Disko was thrice heard to chuckle as Harvey pitched the
split fish into the hold.

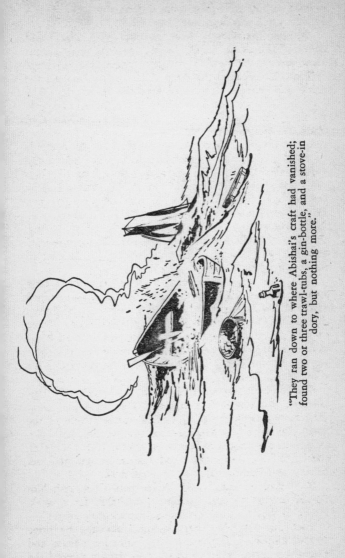

"They ran down to where Abishai's craft had vanished; found two or three trawl-tubs, a gin-bottle, and a stove-in dory, but nothing more."

"Say, you 're haulin' ahead dretful fast," said Dan, when they ground the knives after the men had turned in. "There 's somethin' of a sea to-night, an' I hain't heard you make no remarks on it."

"Too busy," Harvey replied, testing a blade's edge. "Come to think of it, she *is* a high-kicker."

The little schooner was gambolling all around her anchor among the silver-tipped waves. Backing with a start of affected surprise at the sight of the strained cable, she pounced on it like a kitten, while the spray of her descent burst through the hawse-holes with the report of a gun. Shaking her head, she would say: "Well, I 'm sorry I can't stay any longer with you. I 'm going North," and would sidle off, halting suddenly with a dramatic rattle of her rigging. "As I was just going to observe," she would begin, as gravely as a drunken man addressing a lamp-post. The rest of the sentence (she acted her words in dumb-show, of course) was lost in a fit of the fidgets, when she behaved like a puppy chewing a string, a clumsy woman in a side-saddle, a hen with her head cut off, or a cow stung by a hornet, exactly as the whims of the sea took her.

"See her sayin' her piece. She 's Patrick Henry naow," said Dan.

She swung sideways on a roller, and gesticulated with her jib-boom from port to starboard.

"But—ez—fer me, give me liberty—er give me—death!"

Wop! She sat down in the moon-path on the water, courtesying with a flourish of pride impressive enough had not the wheel-gear sniggered mockingly in its box.

Harvey laughed aloud. "Why, it 's just as if she was alive," he said.

"She 's as stiddy as a haouse an' as dry as a herrin'," said Dan enthusiastically, as he was slung across the deck in a batter of spray. "Fends 'em off an' fends 'em off, an' 'Don't ye come anigh me,' she sez. Look at her—jest look at her! Sakes! You should see one o' them toothpicks histin' up her anchor on her spike outer fifteen-fathom water."

"What 's a toothpick, Dan?"

"Them new haddockers an' herrin'-boats. Fine 's a yacht forward, with yacht sterns to 'em, an' spike bowsprits, an' a haouse that 'u'd take our hold. I 've heard that Burgess himself he made the models fer three or four of 'em. Dad 's sot agin 'em on account o' their pitchin' an' joltin', but there 's heaps o' money in 'em. Dad can find fish, but he ain't no ways progressive—he don't go with the march o' the times. They 're chock-full o' labour-savin' jigs an' sech all. 'Ever seed the *Elector* o' Gloucester? She 's a daisy, ef she is a toothpick."

"What do they cost, Dan?"

"Hills o' dollars. Fifteen thousand, p'haps; more, mebbe. There 's gold-leaf an' everything you kin think of." Then to himself, half under his breath, "Guess I 'd call her *Hattie S.*, too."

# CHAPTER V

THAT WAS the first of many talks with Dan, who told Harvey why he would transfer his dory's name to the imaginary Burgess-modelled haddocker. Harvey heard a good deal about the real Hattie at Gloucester; saw a lock of her hair—which Dan, finding fair words of no avail, had "hooked" as she sat in front of him at school that winter—and a photograph. Hattie was about fourteen years old, with an awful contempt for boys, and had been trampling on Dan's heart through the winter. All this was revealed under oath of solemn secrecy on moonlit decks, in the dead dark, or in choking fog; the whining wheel behind them, the climbing deck before, and without, the unresting, clamorous sea. Once, of course, as the boys came to know each other, there was a fight, which raged from bow to stern till Penn came up and separated them, but promised not to tell Disko, who thought fighting on watch rather worse than sleeping. Harvey was no match for Dan physically, but it says a great deal for his new training that he took his defeat and did not try to get even with his conqueror by underhand methods.

That was after he had been cured of a string of boils between his elbows and wrists, where the wet jersey and oilskins cut into the flesh. The salt water stung them unpleasantly, but when they were ripe Dan treated them with Disko's razor, and assured Harvey that now he was a "blooded Banker"; the affliction of gurry-sores being the mark of the caste that claimed him.

Since he was a boy and very busy, he did not bother his head with too much thinking. He was exceedingly sorry for his mother, and often longed to see her and above all to tell her of this wonderful new life, and how brilliantly he was acquitting himself in it. Otherwise he preferred not to wonder too much how she was bearing the shock of his supposed death. But one day, as he stood on the foc'sle ladder, guying the cook, who had accused him and Dan of hooking fried pies, it occurred to him that this was a vast improvement on being snubbed by strangers in the smoking-room of a hired liner.

He was a recognized part of the scheme of things on the *We 'e Here;* had his place at the table and among the bunks; and could hold his own in the long talks on stormy days, when the others were always ready to listen to what they called his "fairy-tales" of his life ashore. It did not take him more than two days and a quarter to feel that if he spoke of his own life—it seemed very far away—no one except Dan (and even Dan's belief was sorely tried) credited him. So he invented a friend, a boy he had heard of, who drove a miniature four-pony drag in Toledo, Ohio, and ordered five suits of clothes at a time and led things called "germans" at parties where the oldest girl was not quite fifteen, but all the presents were solid silver. Salters protested that this kind of yarn was desperately wicked, if not indeed positively blasphemous, but he listened as greedily as the others; and their criticisms at the end gave Harvey entirely new notions on "germans," clothes, cigarettes with gold-leaf tips, rings, watches, scent, small dinner-parties, champagne, card-playing, and hotel accommodation. Little by little he changed his tone when speaking of his "friend," whom Long Jack had christened "the Crazy Kid," "the Gilt-edged Baby," "the Suckin' Vanderpoop," and other pet names; and with his sea-booted feet cocked up on the table would even invent histories about silk pajamas and specially imported neckwear, to the "friend's" discredit. Harvey was a very adaptable person, with a keen eye and ear for every face and tone about him.

Before long he knew where Disko kept the old green-crusted quadrant that they called the "hog-yoke"—under the bed-bag in his bunk. When he took the sun, and with the help of "The Old Farmer's" almanac found the latitude, Harvey would jump down into the cabin and scratch the reckoning and date with a nail on the rust of the stove-pipe. Now, the chief engineer of the liner could have done no more, and no engineer of thirty years' service could have assumed one half of the ancient-mariner air with which Harvey, first careful to spit over the side, made

"A whiteness moved in the whiteness of the fog. It was his first introduction to the dread summer berg of the bank."

public the schooner's position for that day, and then and not till then relieved Disko of the quadrant. There is an etiquette in all these things.

The said "hog-yoke," an Eldridge chart, the farming almanac, Blunt's "Coast Pilot," and Bowditch's "Navigator" were all the weapons Disko needed to guide him, except the deep-sea lead that was his spare eye. Harvey nearly slew Penn with it when Tom Platt taught him first how to "fly the blue pigeon"; and, though his strength was not equal to continuous sounding in any sort of sea, for calm weather with a seven-pound lead on shoal water Disko used him freely. As Dan said: "'T ain't soundin's dad wants. It 's samples. Grease her up good, Harve." Harvey would tallow the cup at the end, and carefully bring the sand, shell, sludge, or whatever it might be, to Disko, who fingered and smelt it and gave judgment. As has been said, when Disko thought of cod he thought as a cod; and by some long-tested mixture of instinct and experience, moved the *We 're Here* from berth to berth, always with the fish, as a blindfolded chess-player moves on the unseen board.

But Disko's board was the Grand Bank—a triangle two hundred and fifty miles on each side—a waste of wallowing sea, cloaked with dank fog, vexed with gales, harried with drifting ice, scored by the tracks of the reckless liners, and dotted with the sails of the fishing-fleet.

For days they worked in fog—Harvey at the bell—till, grown familiar with the thick airs, he went out with Tom Platt, his heart rather in his mouth. But the fog would not lift, and the fish were biting, and no one can stay helplessly afraid for six hours at a time. Harvey devoted himself to his lines and the gaff or gob-stick as Tom Platt called for them; and they rowed back to the schooner guided by the bell and Tom's instinct; Manuel's conch sounding thin and faint beside them. But it was an unearthly experience, and, for the first time in a month, Harvey dreamed of the shifting, smoking floors of water round the dory, the lines that strayed away into nothing, and the air above that melted on the sea below ten feet from his straining eyes. A few days later he was out with Manuel on what should have been forty-fathom bottom, but the whole length of the roding ran out, and still the anchor found nothing, and Harvey grew mortally afraid, for that his last touch with earth was lost. "Whale-hole," said Manuel, hauling in. "That is good joke on Disko. Come!" and he rowed to the schooner to find Tom Platt and the others jeering at the skipper because, for once, he had led them to the edge of the barren Whale-deep, the blank hole of the Grand Bank. They made another berth through the fog, and that time the hair of Harvey's head stood up when he went out in Manuel's dory. A whiteness moved in the whiteness of the fog with a breath like the breath of the grave, and there was a roaring, a plunging, and spouting. It was his first introduction to the dread summer berg of the Banks, and he cowered in the bottom of the boat while Manuel laughed. There were days, though, clear and soft and warm, when it seemed a sin to do anything but loaf over the hand-lines and spank the drifting "sun-scalds" with an oar; and there were days of light airs, when Harvey was taught how to steer the schooner from one berth to another.

It thrilled through him when he first felt the keel answer to his hand on the spokes and slide over the long hollows as the foresail scythed back and forth against the blue sky. That was magnificent, in spite of Disko saying that it would break a snake's back to follow his wake. But, as usual, pride ran before a fall. They were sailing on the wind with the staysail—an old one, luckily—set, and Harvey jammed her right into it to show Dan how completely he had mastered the art. The foresail went over with a bang, and the foregaff stabbed and ripped through the staysail, which was, of course, prevented from going over the mainstay. They lowered the wreck in awful silence, and Harvey spent his leisure hours for the next few days under Tom Platt's lee, learning to use a needle and palm. Dan hooted with joy, for, as he said, he had made the very same blunder himself in his early days.

Boylike, Harvey imitated all the men by turns, till he had combined Disko's peculiar stoop at the wheel, Long Jack's swinging overhand when the lines were hauled, Manuel's round-shouldered but effective stroke in a dory, and Tom Platt's generous *Ohio* stride along the deck.

" 'T is beautiful to see how he takes to ut," said Long

"There were days of light airs, when Harvey was taught how to steer the schooner from one berth to another."

Jack, when Harvey was looking out by the windlass one thick noon. "I 'll lay my wage an' share 't is more 'n half play-actin' to him, an' he consates himself he's a bowld mariner. Watch his little bit av a back now!"

"That 's the way we all begin," said Tom Platt. "The boys they make believe all the time till they 've cheated 'emselves into bein' men, an' so till they die—pretendin' an' pretendin'. I done it on the old *Ohio*, I know. Stood my first watch—harbour-watch—feelin' finer 'n Farragut. Dan 's full o' the same kind o' notions. See 'em now, actin' to be genewine moss-backs every hair a rope-yarn an' blood Stockholm tar." He spoke down the cabin stairs. "Guess you 're mistook in your judgments fer once, Disko. What in Rome made ye tell us all here the kid was crazy?"

"He wuz," Disko replied. "Crazy ez a loon when he come aboard; but I 'll say he 's sobered up consid'ble sence. I cured him."

"He yarns good," said Tom Platt. "T' other night he told us abaout a kid of his own size steerin' a cunnin' little rig an' four ponies up an' down Toledo, Ohio, I think 't was, an' givin' suppers to a crowd o' sim'lar kids. Cur'us kind o' fairy-tale, but blame interestin'. He knows scores of 'em."

"Guess he strikes 'em outen his own head," Disko called from the cabin, where he was busy with the log-book. "Stands to reason that sort is all made up. It don't take in no one but Dan, an' he laughs at it. I 've heard him, behind my back."

"Y' ever hear what Sim'on Peter Ca'houn said when they whacked up a match 'twix' his sister Hitty an' Lorin' Jerauld, an' the boys put up that joke on him daown to Georges?" drawled Uncle Salters, who was dripping peaceably under the lee of the starboard dory-nest.

Tom Platt puffed at his pipe in scornful silence: he was a Cape Cod man, and had not known that tale more than twenty years. Uncle Salters went on with a rasping chuckle:

"Sim'on Peter Ca'houn he said, an' he was jest right, abaout Lorin', 'Ha'af on the taown,' he said, 'an' t' other ha'af blame fool; an' they told me she 's married a 'ich man.' Sim'on Peter Ca'houn he hed n't no roof to his mouth an' talked that way."

"He did n't talk any Pennsylvania Dutch," Tom Platt replied. "You 'd better leave a Cape man to tell that tale. The Ca'houns was gypsies frum 'way back."

"Wal, I don't profess to be any elocutionist," Salters said. "I 'm comin' to the moral o' things. That 's jest abaout what aour Harve be! Ha'af on the taown, an' t' other ha'af blame fool; an' there 's some 'll believe he 's a rich man. Yah!"

"Did ye ever think how sweet 't would be to sail wid a full crew o' Salterses?" said Long Jack. "Ha'af in the furrer an' other ha'af in the muck-heap, as Ca'houn did *not* say, an' makes out he 's a fisherman!"

A little laugh went round at Salters's expense.

Disko held his tongue, and wrought over the log-book that he kept in a hatchet-faced, square hand; this was the kind of thing that ran on, page after soiled page:

*"July 17. This day thick fog and few fish. Made berth to northward. So ends this day.*

*"July 18. This day comes in with thick fog. Caught a few fish.*

*"July 19. This day comes in with light breeze from N.E. and fine weather. Made a berth to eastward. Caught plenty fish.*

*"July 20. This, the Sabbath, comes in with fog and light winds. So ends this day. Total fish caught this week, 3,478."*

They never worked on Sundays, but shaved, and washed themselves if it were fine, and Pennsylvania sang hymns. Once or twice he suggested, that, if it was not an impertinence, he thought he could preach a little. Uncle Salters nearly jumped down his throat at the mere notion, reminding him that he was not a preacher and must n't think of such things. "We 'd hev him rememberin' Johnstown next," Salters explained, "an' what would happen then?" So they compromised on his reading aloud from a book called "Josephus." It was an old leather-bound volume, smelling of a hundred voyages, very solid and very like the Bible, but enlivened with accounts of battles and sieges; and they read it nearly from cover to cover.

Otherwise Penn was a silent little body. He would not utter a word for three days on end sometimes, though he played checkers, listened to the songs, and laughed at the stories. When they tried to stir him up, he would answer: "I don't wish to seem unneighbourly, but it is because I have nothing to say. My head feels quite empty. I 've almost forgotten my name." He would turn to Uncle Salters with an expectant smile.

"Why, Pennsylvania *Pratt*," Salters would shout. "You 'll fergit *me* next!"

"No—never," Penn would say, shutting his lips firmly. "Pennsylvania Pratt, of course," he would repeat over and over. Sometimes it was Uncle Salters who forgot, and told him he was Haskins or Rich or McVitty; but Penn was equally content—till next time.

He was always very tender with Harvey, whom he pitied both as a lost child and as a lunatic; and when Salters saw that Penn liked the boy, he relaxed, too. Salters was not an amiable person (he esteemed it his business to keep the boys in order); and the first time Harvey, in fear and trembling, on a still day, managed to shin up to the main-truck (Dan was behind him ready to help), he esteemed it *his* duty to hang Salters's big sea-boots up there—a sight of shame and derision to the nearest schooner. With Disko, Harvey took no liberties; not even when the old man dropped direct orders, and treated him, like the rest of the crew, to "Don't you want to do so and so?" and "Guess you 'd better," and so forth. There was something about the clean-shaven lips and the puckered corners of the eyes that was mightily sobering to young blood.

Disko showed him the meaning of the thumbed and pricked chart, which, he said, laid over any government publication whatsoever; led him, pencil in hand, from berth to berth over the whole string of banks—Le Have, Western, Banquereau, St. Pierre, Green, and Grand—talking "cod" meantime. Taught him, too, the principle on which the "hog-yoke" was worked.

In this Harvey excelled Dan, for he had inherited a head for figures, and the notion of stealing information from one glimpse of the sullen Bank sun appealed to all his keen wits. For other sea-matters his age handicapped him. As Disko said, he should have begun when he was ten. Dan could bait up trawl or lay his hand on any rope in the dark; and at a pinch, when Uncle Salters had a gurry-sore on his palm, could dress down by sense of touch. He could steer in anything short of half a gale from the feel of the wind on his face, humouring the *We 're Here* just when she needed it. These things he did as automatically as he skipped about the rigging, or made his dory a part of his own will and body. But he could not communicate his knowledge to Harvey.

Still there was a good deal of general information flying about the schooner on stormy days, when they lay up in the foc'sle or sat on the cabin lockers, while spare eye-bolts, leads, and rings rolled and rattled in the pauses of the talk. Disko spoke of whaling voyages in the Fifties; of great she-whales slain beside their young; of death agonies on the black tossing seas, and blood that spurted forty feet in the air; of boats smashed to splinters; of patent rockets that went off wrong-end-first and bombarded the trembling crews; of cutting-in and boiling-down, and that terrible "nip" of '71, when twelve hundred men were made homeless on the ice in three days—wonderful tales, all true. But more wonderful still were his stories of the cod, and how they argued and reasoned on their private businesses deep down below the keel.

Long Jack's tastes ran more to the supernatural. He held them silent with ghastly stories of the "Yo-hoes" on Monomoy Beach, that mock and terrify lonely clam-diggers; of sand-walkers and dune-haunters who were never properly buried; of hidden treasure on Fire Island guarded by the spirits of Kidd's men; of ships that sailed in the fog straight over Truro township; of that harbour in Maine where no one but a stranger will lie at anchor twice in a certain place because of a dead crew who row along-side at midnight with the anchor in the bow of their old-fashioned boat, whistling—not calling, but whistling—for the soul of the man who broke their rest.

Harvey had a notion that the east coast of his native land, from Mount Desert south, was populated chiefly by people who took their horses there in the summer and entertained in country-houses with hardwood floors and

Vantine portières. He laughed at the ghost-tales,—not as much as he would have done a month before,—but ended by sitting still and shuddering.

Tom Platt dealt with his interminable trip round the Horn on the old *Ohio* in the flogging days, with a navy more extinct than the dodo—the navy that passed away in the great war. He told them how red-hot shot are dropped into a cannon, a wad of wet clay between them and the cartridge; how they sizzle and reek when they strike wood, and how the little ship-boys of the *Miss Jim Buck* hove water over them and shouted to the fort to try again. And he told tales of blockade—long weeks of swaying at anchor, varied only by the departure and return of steamers that had used up their coal (there was no chance for the sailing-ships); of gales and cold—cold that kept two hundred men, night and day, pounding and chopping at the ice on cable, blocks, and rigging, when the galley was as red-hot as the fort's shot, and men drank cocoa by the bucket. Tom Platt had no use for steam. His service closed when that thing was comparatively new. He admitted that it was a specious invention in time of peace, but looked hopefully for the day when sails should come back again on ten-thousand-ton frigates with hundred-and-ninety-foot booms.

Manuel's talk was slow and gentle—all about pretty girls in Madeira washing clothes in the dry beds of streams, by moonlight, under waving bananas; legends of saints, and tales of queer dances or fights away in the cold Newfoundland baiting-ports. Salters was mainly agricultural; for, though he read "Josephus" and expounded it, his mission in life was to prove the value of green manures, and specially of clover, against every form of phosphate whatsoever. He grew libellous about phosphates; he dragged greasy "Orange Judd" books from his bunk and intoned them, wagging his finger at Harvey, to whom it was all Greek. Little Penn was so genuinely pained when Harvey made fun of Salters's lectures that the boy gave it up, and suffered in polite silence. That was very good for Harvey.

The cook naturally did not join in these conversations. As a rule, he spoke only when it was absolutely necessary; but at times a queer gift of speech descended on him, and he held forth, half in Gaelic, half in broken English, an hour at a time. He was especially communicative with the boys, and he never withdrew his prophecy that one day Harvey would be Dan's master, and that he would see it. He told them of mail-carrying in the winter up Cape Breton way, of the dog-train that goes to Coudray, and of the ram-steamer *Arctic*, that breaks the ice between the mainland and Prince Edward Island. Then he told them stories that his mother had told him, of life far to the southward, where water never froze; and he said that when he died his soul would go to lie down on a warm white beach of sand with palm-trees waving above. That seemed to the boys a very odd idea for a man who had never seen a palm in his life. Then, too, regularly at each meal, he would ask Harvey, and Harvey alone, whether the cooking was to his taste; and this always made the "second half" laugh. Yet they had a great respect for the cook's judgment, and in their hearts considered Harvey something of a mascot by consequence.

And while Harvey was taking in knowledge of new things at each pore and hard health with every gulp of the good air, the *We 're Here* went her ways and did her business on the Bank, and the silvery-gray kenches of well-pressed fish mounted higher and higher in the hold. No one day's work was out of common, but the average days were many and close together.

Naturally, a man of Disko's reputation was closely watched—"scrowged upon," Dan called it—by his neighbours, but he had a very pretty knack of giving them the slip through the curdling, glidy fog-banks. Disko avoided company for two reasons. He wished to make his own experiments, in the first place; and in the second, he objected to the mixed gatherings of a fleet of all nations. The bulk of them were mainly Gloucester boats, with a scattering from Provincetown, Harwich, Chatham, and some of the Maine ports, but the crews drew from goodness knows where. Risk breeds recklessness, and when greed is added there are fine chances for every kind of accident in the crowded fleet, which, like a mob of sheep, is huddled round some unrecognized leader. "Let the two Jeraulds lead 'em," said Disko. "We 're baound to lay among 'em for a spell on the Eastern Shoals; though ef luck holds, we won't hev to lay long. Where we are naow, Harve, ain't considered noways good graound."

"Ain't it?" said Harvey, who was drawing water (he had learned just how to wiggle the bucket), after an unusually long dressing-down. "Should n't mind striking some poor ground for a change, then."

"All the graound I want to see—don't want to strike her—is Eastern Point," said Dan. "Say, Dad, it looks 's if we would n't hev to lay more 'n two weeks on the Shoals. You 'll meet all the comp'ny you want then, Harve. That 's the time we begin to work. No reg'lar meals fer no one then. 'Mug-up when ye 're hungry, an' sleep when ye can't keep awake. Good job you was n't picked up a month later than you was, or we 'd never ha' had you dressed in shape fer the Old Virgin."

Harvey understood from the Eldridge chart that the Old Virgin and a nest of curiously named shoals were the turning-point of the cruise, and that with good luck they would wet the balance of their salt there. But seeing the size of the Virgin (it was one tiny dot), he wondered how even Disko with the hog-yoke and the lead could find her. He learned later that Disko was entirely equal to that and any other business and could even help others. A big four-by-five blackboard hung in the cabin, and Harvey never understood the need of it till, after some blinding thick days, they heard the unmelodious tooting of a foot-power fog-horn—a machine whose note is as that of a consumptive elephant.

They were making a short berth, towing the anchor under their foot to save trouble. "Square-rigger bellowin' fer his latitude," said Long Jack. The dripping red head-sails of a bark glided out of the fog, and the *We 're Here* rang her bell thrice, using sea shorthand.

The larger boat backed her topsail with shrieks and shoutings.

"Frenchman," said Uncle Salters, scornfully. "Miquelon boat from St. Malo." The farmer had a weatherly sea-eye. "I 'm 'most outer 'baccy, too, Disko."

"Same here!" said Tom Platt. "Hi! *Backez vous—backez vous! Standez awayez,* you butt-ended *mucho-bono!* Where you from—St. Malo, eh?"

"Ah, ha! *Mucho bono! Oui! oui! Clos Poulet—St. Malo!*

*St. Pierre et Miquelon,"* cried the other crowd, waving
woollen caps and laughing. Then all together, *"Bord!
Bord!"*

"Bring up the board, Danny. Beats me how them Frenchmen fetch anywheres, exceptin' America's fairish broadly.
Forty-six forty-nine's good enough fer them; an' I guess
it 's abaout right, too."

Dan chalked the figures on the board, and they hung
it in the main-rigging to a chorus of *mercis* from the bark.

"Seems kinder unneighbourly to let 'em swedge off
like this," Salters suggested, feeling in his pockets.

"Hev ye learned French then sence last trip?" said
Disko. *"I* don't want no more stone-ballast hove at us 'long
o' your callin' Miquelon boats 'footy cochins,' same 's you
did off Le Have."

"Harmon Rush he said that was the way to rise 'em.
Plain United States is good enough fer me. We 're all
dretful short on terbakker. Young feller, don't *you* speak
French?"

"Oh, yes," said Harvey valiantly; and he bawled: "Hi!
Say! *Arrêtez vous! Attendez! Nous sommes venant pour
tabac."*

"Ah, *tabac, tabac!"* they cried, and laughed again.

"That hit 'em. Let's heave a dory over, anyway," said
Tom Platt. "I don't exactly hold no certificates on French,
but I know another lingo that goes, I guess. Come on,
Harve, an' interpret."

The raffle and confusion when he and Harvey were
hauled up the bark's black side was indescribable. Her
cabin was all stuck round with glaring coloured prints of
the Virgin—the Virgin of Newfoundland, they called her.
Harvey found his French of no recognized Bank brand,
and his conversation was limited to nods and grins. But
Tom Platt waved his arms and got along swimmingly.
The captain gave him a drink of unspeakable gin, and the
opéra-comique crew, with their hairy throats, red caps, and
long knives, greeted him as a brother. Then the trade
began. They had tobacco, plenty of it—American, that had
never paid duty to France. They wanted chocolate and
crackers. Harvey rowed back to arrange with the cook and
Disko, who owned the stores, and on his return the cocoa-
tins and cracker-bags were counted out by the Frenchman's

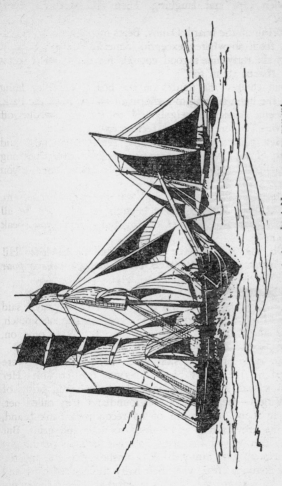

"Hi! Say! Arrêtez vous! Attendez! Nous sommes venant pour tabac.' 'Ah, tabac, tabac!'"

wheel. It looked like a piratical division of loot; but Tom Platt came out of it roped with black pigtail and stuffed with cakes of chewing and smoking tobacco. Then those jovial mariners swung off into the mist, and the last Harvey heard was a gay chorus:

> "Par derrière chez ma tante,
> Il y a un bois joli,
> Et le rossignol y chante
> Et le jour et la nuit . . .
>
> Que donneriez vous, belle,
> Qui l'amènerait ici?
> Je donnerai Québec,
> Sorel et Saint Denis."

"How was it my French did n't go, and your sign-talk did?" Harvey demanded when the barter had been distributed among the *We 're Heres.*

"Sign-talk!" Platt guffawed. "Well, yes, 't was sign-talk, but a heap older 'n your French, Harve. Them French boats are chock-full o' Freemasons, an' that 's why."

"Are you a Freemason, then?"

"Looks that way, don't it?" said the man-o'-war's man, stuffing his pipe; and Harvey had another mystery of the deep sea to brood upon.

# CHAPTER VI

THE THING that struck him most was the exceedingly casual way in which some craft loafed about the broad Atlantic. Fishing-boats, as Dan said, were naturally dependent on the courtesy and wisdom of their neighbours; but one expected better things of steamers. That was after another interesting interview, when they had been chased for three miles by a big lumbering old cattle-boat, all boarded over on the upper deck, that smelt like a thousand cattle-pens. A very excited officer yelled at them through a speaking-trumpet, and she lay and lollopped helplessly on the water while Disko ran the *We 're Here* under her lee and gave the skipper a piece of his mind. "Where might ye be—eh? Ye don't deserve to be anywheres. You barn-yard tramps go hoggin' the road on the high seas with no blame consideration fer your neighbours, an' your eyes in your coffee-cups instid o' in your silly heads."

At this the skipper danced on the bridge and said something about Disko's own eyes. "We have n't had an observation for three days. D' you suppose we can run her blind?" he shouted.

"Wa-al, *I* can," Disko retorted. "What 's come to your lead? Et it? Can't ye smell bottom, or are them cattle too rank?"

"What d' ye feed 'em?" said Uncle Salters with intense seriousness, for the smell of the pens woke all the farmer in him. "They say they fall off dretful on a v'yage. Dunno as it 's any o' my business, but I 've a kind o' notion that oil-cake broke small an' sprinkled——"

"Thunder!" said a cattle-man in a red jersey as he looked over the side. "What asylum did they let His Whiskers out of"

"Young feller," Salters began, standing up in the fore-rigging, "let me tell *yeou* 'fore we go any further that I 've——"

86

The officer on the bridge took off his cap with immense politeness. "Excuse me," he said, "but I 've asked for my reckoning. If the agricultural person with the hair will kindly shut his head, the sea-green barnacle with the wall-eye may per-haps condescend to enlighten us."

"Naow you 've made a show o' me, Salters," said Disko, angrily. He could not stand up to that particular sort of talk, and snapped out the latitude and longitude without more lectures.

"Well, that 's a boat-load of lunatics, sure," said the skipper, as he rang up the engine-room and tossed a bundle of newspapers into the schooner.

"Of *all* the blamed fools, next to you, Salters, him an' his crowd are abaout the likeliest I 've ever seen," said Disko as the *We 're Here* slid away. "I was jest givin' him my jedgment on lullsikin' round these waters like a lost child, an' you must cut in with your fool farmin'. Can't ye never keep things sep'rate?"

Harvey, Dan, and the others stood back, winking one to the other and full of joy; but Disko and Salters wrangled seriously till evening, Salters arguing that a cattle-boat was practically a barn on blue water, and Disko insisting that, even if this were the case, decency and fisher-pride demanded that he should have kept "things sep'-rate." Long Jack stood it in silence for a time,—an angry skipper makes an unhappy crew,—and then he spoke across the table after supper:

"Fwhat 's the good o' bodderin' fwhat they 'll say?" said he.

"They 'll tell that tale agin us fer years—that 's all," said Disko. "Oil-cake sprinkled!"

"With salt, o' course," said Salters, impenitent, reading the farming reports from a week-old New York paper.

"It 's plumb mortifyin' to all my feelin's," the skipper went on.

"Can't see ut that way," said Long Jack, the peace-maker. "Look at here, Disko! Is there another packet afloat this day in this weather cud ha' met a tramp an', over an' above givin' her her reckonin',—over an' above that, I say,—cud ha' discoorsed wid her quite intelligent on the manage-ment av steers an' such at sea? Forgit ut! Av coorse they will not. 'T was the most compenjus conversation that iver accrued. Double game an' twice runnin'—all to us." Dan kicked Harvey under the table, and Harvey choked in his cup.

"Well," said Salters, who felt that his honour had been somewhat plastered. "I *said* I did n't know as 't wuz any business o' mine, 'fore I spoke."

"An' right there," said Tom Platt, experienced in discipline and etiquette—"right there, I take it, Disko, you should ha' asked him to stop ef the conversation wuz likely, in your jedgment, to be anyways—what it should n't."

" 'Dunno but that 's so," said Disko, who saw his way to an honourable retreat from a fit of the dignities.

"Why, o' course it was so," said Salters, "you bein' skipper here; an' I 'd cheerful hev stopped on a hint—not from any leadin' *or* conviction, but fer the sake o' bearin' an example to these two blame boys of aours."

"Did n't I tell you, Harve, 't would come araound to us 'fore we 'd done? Always those blame boys. But I would n't have missed the show fer a half-share in a halibutter," Dan whispered.

"*Still,* things should ha' been kep' sep'rate," said Disko, and the light of new argument lit in Salters's eye as he crumbled cut plug into his pipe.

"There 's a power av vartue in keepin' things sep'rate," said Long Jack, intent on stilling the storm. "That 's fwhat Steyning of Steyning and Hare's f'und when he sent Counahan fer skipper on the *Marilla D. Kuhn,* instid o' Cap. Newton that was took with inflam'try rheumatism an' could n't go. Counahan the Navigator we called him."

"Nick Counahan he never went aboard fer a night 'thout a pond o' rum somewheres in the manifest," said Tom Platt, playing up to the lead. "He used to bum araound the c'mission houses to Boston lookin' fer the Lord to make him captain of a tow-boat on his merits. Sam Coy, up to Atlantic Avenoo, give him his board free fer a year or more on account of his stories. Counahan the Navigator! Tck! Tck! Dead these fifteen year, ain't he?"

"Seventeen, I guess. He died the year the *Caspar Mc-Veagh* was built; but he could niver keep things sep'rate. Steyning tuk him fer the reason the thief tuk the hot stove —bekaze there was nothin' else that season. The men was all to the Banks, and Counahan he whacked up an iver-

lastin' hard crowd fer crew. Rum! Ye cud ha' floated the
*Marilla*, insurance an' all, in fwhat they stowed aboard her.
They lef' Boston Harbour for the great Grand Bank wid
a roarin' nor'wester behind 'em an' all hands full to the
bung. An' the hivens looked after thim, for divil a watch
did they set, an' divil a rope did they lay hand to, till they'd
seen the bottom av a fifteen-gallon cask o' bug-juice. That
was about wan week, so far as Counahan remembered. (If
I cud only tell the tale as he told ut!) All that whoile the
wind blew like ould glory, an' the *Marilla*—'t was summer,
and they'd give her a foretopmast—struck her gait and kept
ut. Then Counahan tuk the hog-yoke an' thrembled over it
for a while, an' made out, betwix' that an' the chart an' the
singin' in his head, that they was to be south'ard o' Sable
Island, gettin' along glorious, but speakin' nothin'. Then
they broached another keg, an' quit speculatin' about anythin' fer another spell. The *Marilla* she lay down whin she
dropped Boston Light, and she never lufted her lee-rail
up to that time—hustlin' on one an' the same slant. But
they saw no weed, nor gulls, nor schooners; an' prisintly
they observed they 'd bin out a matter o' fourteen days
and they mistrusted the Bank has suspinded payment. So
they sounded, an' got sixty fathom. 'That 's me,' sez Counahan. 'That 's me iv'ry time! I 've run her slat on the Bank
fer you, an' when we get thirty fathom we 'll turn in like
little men. Counahan is the b'y,' sez he. 'Counahan the
Navigator!'

"Nex' cast they got ninety. Sez Counahan: 'Either the
lead-line 's tuk to stretchin' or else the Bank 's sunk.'

"They hauled ut up, bein' just about in that state when ut
seemed right an' reasonable, and sat down on the deck
countin' the knots, an' gettin' her snarled up hijjus. The
*Marilla* she 'd struck her gait, an' she hild ut, an' prisintly
along come a tramp, an' Counahan spoke her.

"'Hev ye seen any fishin'-boats now?' sez he, quite casual.

"'There 's lashin's av them off the Irish coast,' sez the
tramp.

"'Aah! go shake yerself,' sez Counahan. 'Fwhat have I to
do wid the Irish coast?'

"'Then fwhat are ye doin' here?' sez the tramp.

"'Sufferin' Christianity!' sez Counahan (he always said

that whin his pumps sucked an' he was not feelin' good)—
'Sufferin' Christianity!' he sez, 'where am I at?'

" 'Thirty-five mile west-sou'west o' Cape Clear,' sez the
tramp, 'if that 's any consolation to you.'

"Counahan fetched wan jump, four feet sivin inches,
measured by the cook.

" 'Consolation!' sez he, bould as brass. 'D' ye take me fer a
dialect? Thirty-five mile from Cape Clear, an' fourteen days
from Boston Light. Sufferin' Christianity, 't is a record, an'
by the same token I 've a mother to Skibbereen!' Think av
ut! The gall av um! But ye see he could niver keep things
sep'rate.

"The crew was mostly Cork an' Kerry men, barrin' one
Marylander that wanted to go back, but they called him a
mutineer, an' they ran the ould *Marilla* into Skibbereen, an'
they had an illigant time visitin' around with frinds on the
ould sod fer a week. Thin they wint back, an' it cost 'em two
an' thirty days to beat to the Banks again. 'T was gettin' on
towards fall, and grub was low, so Counahan ran her back
to Boston, wid no more bones to ut."

"And what did the firm say?" Harvey demanded.

"Fwhat could they? The fish was on the Banks, an' Counahan was at T-wharf talkin' av his record trip east! They tuk
their satisfaction out av that, an' ut all came av not keepin'
the crew and the rum sep'rate in the first place; an' confusin'
Skibbereen wid 'Queereau, in the second. Counahan the
Navigator, rest his sowl! He was an impromptu citizen!"

"Once I was in the *Lucy Holmes*," said Manuel, in his
gentle voice. "They not want any of her feesh in Gloucester.
Eh, wha-at? Give us no price. So we go across the water, and
think to sell to some Fayal man. Then it blow fresh, and we
cannot see well. Eh, wha-at? Then it blow some more fresh,
and we go down below and drive very fast—no one knows
where. By and by we see a land, and it get some hot. Then
come two, three nigger in a brick. Eh, wha-at? We ask
where we are, and they say—now, what you all think?"

"Grand Canary," said Disko, after a moment. Manuel
shook his head, smiling.

"Blanco," said Tom Platt.

"No. Worse than that. We was below Bezagos, and the
brick she was from Liberia! So we sell our feesh *there*! Not
bad, so? Eh, wha-at?"

"Can a schooner like this go right across to Africa?" said Harvey.

"Go araound the Horn ef there's anythin' worth goin' fer, and the grub holds aout," said Disko. "My father he run his packet, an' she was a kind o' pinkey, abaout fifty ton, I guess, —the *Rupert*,—he run her over to Greenland's icy mountains the year ha'af our fleet was tryin' after cod there. An' what's more, he took my mother along with him,—to show her haow the money was earned, I presoom,—an' they was all iced up, an' I was born at Disko. Don't remember nothin' abaout it, o' course. We come back when the ice eased in the spring, but they named me fer the place. Kinder mean trick to put up on a baby, but we're all baound to make mistakes in aour lives."

"Sure! Sure!" said Salters, wagging his head. "All baound to make mistakes, an' I tell you two boys here thet after you've made a mistake—ye don't make fewer 'n a hundred a day—the next best thing's to own up to it like men."

Long Jack winked one tremendous wink that embraced all hands except Disko and Salters, and the incident was closed.

Then they made berth after berth to the northward, the dories out almost every day, running along the east edge of the Grand Bank in thirty- to forty-fathom water, and fishing steadily.

It was here Harvey first met the squid, who is one of the best cod-baits, but uncertain in his moods. They were waked out of their bunks one black night by yells of "Squid O!" from Salters, and for an hour and a half every soul aboard hung over his squid-jig—a piece of lead painted red and armed at the lower end with a circle of pins bent backward like half-opened umbrella ribs. The squid—for some unknown reason—likes, and wraps himself round, this thing, and is hauled up ere he can escape from the pins. But as he leaves his home he squirts first water and next ink into his captor's face; and it was curious to see the men weaving their heads from side to side to dodge the shot. They were as black as sweeps when the flurry ended; but a pile of fresh squid lay on the deck, and the large cod thinks very well of a little shiny piece of squid tentacle at the tip of a clam-baited hook. Next day they caught many fish, and met the *Carrie Pitman,* to whom they shouted their luck, and she wanted to trade—seven cod for one fair-sized squid; but Disko would not agree at the price, and the *Carrie* dropped sullenly to leeward and anchored half a mile away, in the hope of striking on to some for herself.

Disko said nothing till after supper, when he sent Dan and Manuel out to buoy the *We 're Here's* cable and announced his intention of turning in with the broad-axe. Dan naturally repeated these remarks to a dory from the *Carrie,* who wanted to know why they were buoying their cable, since they were not on rocky bottom.

"Dad sez he would n't trust a ferryboat within five mile o' you," Dan howled cheerfully.

"Why don't he git out, then? Who 's hinderin'?" said the other.

"'Cause you 've jest the same ez lee-bowed him, an' he don't take that from any boat, not to speak o' sech a driftin' gurry-butt as you be."

"She ain't driftin' any this trip," said the man angrily, for the *Carrie Pitman* had an unsavory reputation for breaking her ground-tackle.

"Then haow d' you make berths?" said Dan. "It 's her best p'int o' sailin'. An' ef she's quit driftin', what in thunder are you doin' with a new jib-boom?" That shot went home.

"Hey, you Portugoosy organ-grinder, take your monkey back to Gloucester. Go back to school, Dan Troop," was the answer.

"O-ver-alls! O-ver-alls!" yelled Dan, who knew that one of the *Carrie's* crew had worked in an overall factory the winter before.

"Shrimp! Gloucester shrimp! Git aout, you Novy!"

To call a Gloucester man a Nova Scotian is not well received. Dan answered in kind.

"Novy yourself, ye Scrabble-towners! ye Chatham wreckers! Git aout with your brick in your stockin'!" And the forces separated, but Chatham had the worst of it.

"I knew haow 't would be," said Disko. "She's drawed the wind raound already. Some one oughter put a *dee*sist on thet packet. She'll snore till midnight, an' jest when we're gettin' our sleep she'll strike adrift. Good job we ain't crowded with craft hereaways. But I ain't goin' to up anchor fer Chatham. She may hold."

The wind, which had hauled round, rose at sundown and

blew steadily. There was not enough sea, though, to disturb even a dory's tackle, but the *Carrie Pitman* was a law unto herself. At the end of the boys' watch they heard the *crack-crack-crack* of a huge muzzle-loading revolver aboard her.

"Glory, glory, hallelujah!" sung Dan. "Here she comes, Dad; butt-end first, walkin' in her sleep same 's she done on 'Queereau."

Had she been any other boat Disko would have taken his chances, but now he cut the cable as the *Carrie Pitman,* with all the North Atlantic to play in, lurched down directly upon them. The *We 're Here,* under jib and riding-sail, gave her no more room than was absolutely necessary,—Disko did not wish to spend a week hunting for his cable,—but scuttled up into the wind as the *Carrie* passed within easy hail, a silent and angry boat, at the mercy of a raking broad-side of Bank chaff.

"Good evenin'," said Disko, raising his head-gear, "an' haow does your garden grow?"

"Go to Ohio an' hire a mule," said Uncle Salters. "We don't want no farmers here."

"Will I lend you my dory-anchor?" cried Long Jack.

"Unship your rudder an' stick it in the mud," said Tom Platt.

"Say!" Dan's voice rose shrill and high, as he stood on the wheel-box. "Sa-ay! Is there a strike in the o-ver-all factory; or hev they hired girls, ye Shackamaxons?"

"Veer out the tiller-lines," cried Harvey, "and nail 'em to the bottom." That was a salt-flavoured jest he had been put up to by Tom Platt. Manuel leaned over the stern and yelled: "Johanna Morgan play the organ! Ahaaaa!" He flourished his broad thumb with a gesture of unspeakable contempt and derision, while little Penn covered himself with glory by piping up: "Gee a little! Hssh! Come here. Haw!"

They rode on their chain for the rest of the night, a short, snappy, uneasy motion, as Harvey found, and wasted half the forenoon recovering the cable. But the boys agreed the trouble was cheap at the price of triumph and glory, and they thought with grief over all the beautiful things that they might have said to the discomfited *Carrie.*

# CHAPTER VII

NEXT DAY they fell in with more sails, all circling slowly from the east northerly towards the west. But just when they expected to make the shoals by the Virgin the fog shut down, and they anchored, surrounded by the tinklings of invisible bells. There was not much fishing, but occasionally dory met dory in the fog and exchanged news.

That night, a little before dawn, Dan and Harvey, who had been sleeping most of the day, tumbled out to "hook" fried pies. There was no reason why they should not have taken them openly; but they tasted better so, and it made the cook angry. The heat and smell below drove them on deck with their plunder, and they found Disko at the bell, which he handed over to Harvey.

"Keep her goin'," said he. "I mistrust I hear somethin'. Ef it 's anything, I 'm best where I am so 's to get at things."

It was a forlorn little jingle; the thick air seemed to pinch it off; and in the pauses Harvey heard the muffled shriek of a liner's siren, and he knew enough of the Banks to know what that meant. It came to him, with horrible distinctness, how a boy in a cherry-coloured jersey—he despised fancy blazers now with all a fisherman's contempt—how an ignorant, rowdy boy had once said it would be "great" if a steamer ran down a fishing-boat. That boy had a stateroom with a hot and cold bath, and spent ten minutes each morning picking over a gilt-edged bill of fare. And that same boy —no, his very much older brother—was up at four of the dim dawn in streaming, crackling oilskins, hammering, literally for the dear life, on a bell smaller than the steward's breakfast-bell, while somewhere close at hand a thirty-foot steel stem was storming along at twenty miles an hour! The bitterest thought of all was that there were folks asleep in dry, upholstered cabins who would never learn that they had massacred a boat before breakfast. So Harvey rang the bell.

"Yes, they slow daown one turn o' their blame propeller," said Dan, applying himself to Manuel's conch, "fer to keep inside the law, an' that 's consolin' when we 're all at the bottom. Hark to her! She 's a humper!"

"*Aoooo—whoooo—whupp!*" went the siren. "*Wingle—tingle—tink,*" went the bell. "*Graaa—ouch!*" went the conch, while sea and sky were all milled up in milky fog. Then Harvey felt that he was near a moving body, and found himself looking up and up at the wet edge of a cliff-like bow, leaping, it seemed, directly over the schooner. A jaunty little feather of water curled in front of it, and as it lifted it showed a long ladder of Roman numerals—XV., XVI., XVII., XVIII., and so forth—on a salmon-coloured gleaming side. It tilted forward and downward with a heart-stilling "Ssssooo"; the ladder disappeared; a line of brass-rimmed port-holes flashed past; a jet of steam puffed in Harvey's helplessly uplifted hands; a spout of hot water roared along the rail of the *We 're Here,* and the little schooner staggered and shook in a rush of screw-torn water, as a liner's stern vanished in the fog. Harvey got ready to faint or be sick, or both, when he heard a crack like a trunk thrown on a sidewalk, and, all small in his ear, a far-away telephone voice drawling: "Heave to! You 've sunk us!"

"Is it us?" he gasped.

"No! Boat out yonder. Ring! We're goin' to look," said Dan, running out a dory.

In half a minute all except Harvey, Penn, and the cook were overside and away. Presently a schooner's stump-fore-mast, snapped clean across, drifted past the bows. Then an empty green dory came by, knocking on the *We 're Here's* side, as though she wished to be taken in. Then followed something, face down, in a blue jersey, but—it was not the whole of a man. Penn changed colour and caught his breath with a click. Harvey pounded despairingly at the bell, for he feared they might be sunk at any minute, and he jumped at Dan's hail as the crew came back.

"The *Jennie Cushman,*" said Dan, hysterically, "cut clean in half—graound up an' trompled on at that! Not a quarter of a mile away. Dad 's got the old man. There ain't any one else, and—there was his son, too. Oh, Harve, Harve, I can't stand it! I 've seen——" He dropped his head on his arms and sobbed while the others dragged a gray-headed man aboard.

"What did you pick me up for?" the stranger groaned. "Disko, what did you pick me up for?"

Disko dropped a heavy hand on his shoulder, for the man's eyes were wild and his lips trembled as he stared at the silent crew. Then up and spoke Pennsylvania Pratt, who was also Haskins or Rich or McVitty when Uncle Salters forgot; and his face was changed on him from the face of a fool to the countenance of an old, wise man, and he said in a strong voice: "The Lord gave, and the Lord hath taken away; blessed be the name of the Lord! I was—I am a minister of the Gospel. Leave him to me."

"Oh, you be, be you?" said the man. "Then pray my son back to me! Pray back a nine-thousand-dollar boat an' a thousand quintal of fish. If you'd left me alone my widow could ha' gone on to the Provident an' worked fer her board, an' never known—an' never known. Now I 'll hev to tell her."

"There ain't nothin' to say," said Disko. "Better lie down a piece, Jason Olley."

When a man has lost his only son, his summer's work, and his means of livelihood, in thirty counted seconds, it is hard to give consolation.

"All Gloucester men, was n't they?" said Tom Platt, fiddling helplessly with a dory-becket.

"Oh, *that* don't make no odds," said Jason, wringing the wet from his beard. "I 'll be rowin' summer boarders araound East Gloucester this fall." He rolled heavily to the rail, singing:

> "Happy birds that sing and fly
> Round thine altars, O Most High!"

"Come with me. Come below!" said Penn, as though he had a right to give orders. Their eyes met and fought for a quarter of a minute.

"I dunno who you be, but I 'll come," said Jason submissively. "Mebbe I 'll get back some o' the—some o' the—nine thousand dollars." Penn led him into the cabin and slid the door behind.

"That ain't Penn," cried Uncle Salters. "It's Jacob Boller, an'—he 's remembered Johnstown! I never seed such eyes in any livin' man's head. What's to do naow? What'll I do naow?"

They could hear Penn's voice and Jason's together. Then Penn's went on alone, and Salters slipped off his hat, for Penn was praying. Presently the little man came up the steps, huge drops of sweat on his face, and looked at the crew. Dan was still sobbing by the wheel.

"He don't know us," Salters groaned. "It's all to do over again, checkers and everything—an' what'll he say to *me?*"

Penn spoke; they could hear that it was to strangers. "I have prayed," said he. "Our people believe in prayer. I have prayed for the life of this man's son. Mine were drowned before my eyes—she and my eldest and—the others. Shall a man be more wise than his Maker? I prayed never for their lives, but I have prayed for this man's son, and he will surely be sent him."

Salters looked pleadingly at Penn to see if he remembered.

"How long have I been mad?" Penn asked suddenly. His mouth was twitching.

"Pshaw, Penn! You were n't never mad," Salters began. "Only a little distracted like."

"I saw the houses strike the bridge before the fires broke out. I do not remember any more. How long ago is that?"

"I can't stand it! I can't stand it!" cried Dan, and Harvey whimpered in sympathy.

"Abaout five year," said Disko, in a shaking voice.

"Then I have been a charge on some one for every day of that time. Who was the man?"

Disko pointed to Salters.

"Ye hain't—ye hain't!" cried the sea-farmer, twisting his hands together. "Ye 've more 'n earned your keep twice-told; an' there 's money owin' you, Penn, besides ha'af o' my quarter-share in the boat, which is yours fer value received."

"You are good men. I can see that in your faces. But——"

"Mother av Mercy," whispered Long Jack, "an' he 's been wid us all these trips! He's clean bewitched."

A schooner's bell struck up alongside, and a voice hailed through the fog: "O Disko! 'Heard abaout the *Jennie Cushman?*"

"They have found his son," cried Penn. "Stand you still and see the salvation of the Lord!"

"Got Jason aboard here," Disko answered, but his voice quavered. "There—war n't any one else?"

"We 've f'und one, though. Run acrost him snarled up in a mess o' lumber that might ha' bin a foc'sle. His head 's cut some."

"Who is he?"

The *We 're Here's* heart-beats answered one another.

"Guess it 's young Olley," the voice drawled.

Penn raised his hands and said something in German. Harvey could have sworn that a bright sun was shining upon his lifted face; but the drawl went on: "Sa-ay! You fellers guyed us consid'rable t' other night."

"We don't feel like guyin' any now," said Disko.

"I know it; but to tell the honest truth we was kinder— kinder driftin' when we run agin young Olley."

It was the irrepressible *Carrie Pitman,* and a roar of unsteady laughter went up from the deck of the *We 're Here.*

"Hed n't you 'baout's well send the old man aboard? We 're runnin' in fer more bait an' graound-tackle. Guess you won't want him, anyway, an' this blame windlass work makes us short-handed. We 'll take care of him. He married my woman's aunt."

"I 'll give you anything in the boat," said Troop.

"Don't want nothin', 'less, mebbe, an anchor that 'll hold. Say! Young Olley 's gittin' kinder baulky an' excited. Send the old man along."

Penn waked him from his stupor of despair, and Tom Platt rowed him over. He went away without a word of thanks, not knowing what was to come; and the fog closed over all.

"And now," said Penn, drawing a deep breath as though about to preach. "And now"—the erect body sank like a sword driven home into the scabbard; the light faded from the overbright eyes; the voice returned to its usual pitiful little titter—"and now," said Pennsylvania Pratt, "do you think it's too early for a little game of checkers, Mr. Salters?"

"The very thing—the very thing I was goin' to say myself," cried Salters promptly. "It beats all, Penn, how ye git on to what's in a man's mind."

The little fellow blushed and meekly followed Salters forward.

"Up anchor! Hurry! Let's quit these crazy waters," shouted Disko, and never was he more swiftly obeyed.

"Now what in creation d 'ye suppose is the meanin' o' that all?" said Long Jack, when they were working through the fog once more, damp, dripping, and bewildered.

"The way I sense it," said Disko, at the wheel, "is this: The *Jennie Cushman* business comin' on an empty stummick——"

"He—we saw one of them go by," sobbed Harvey.

"An' *that*, o' course, kinder hove him outer water, julluk runnin' a craft ashore; hove him right aout, I take it, to rememberin' Johnstown an' Jacob Boller an' such-like reminiscences. Well, consolin' Jason there held him up a piece, same's shorin' up a boat. Then, bein' weak, them props slipped an' slipped, an' he slided down the ways, an' naow he's water-borne agin. That 's haow I sense it."

They decided that Disko was entirely correct.

" 'T would ha' bruk Salters all up," said Long Jack, "if Penn had stayed Jacob Bollerin'. Did ye see his face when Penn asked who he 'd been charged on all these years? How is ut, Salters?"

"Asleep—dead asleep. Turned in like a child," Salters replied, tiptoeing aft. "There won't be no grub till he wakes, natural. Did ye ever see sech a gift in prayer? He everlastin'ly hiked young Olley outer the ocean. Thet's my belief. Jason was tur'ble praoud of his boy, an' I mistrusted all along 't was a jedgment on worshippin' vain idols."

"There 's others jest as sot," said Disko.

"That 's dif'runt," Salters retorted quickly. "Penn 's not all caulked, an' I ain't only but doin' my duty by him."

They waited, those hungry men, three hours, till Penn reappeared with a smooth face and a blank mind. He said he believed that he had been dreaming. Then he wanted to know why they were so silent, and they could not tell him.

Disko worked all hands mercilessly for the next four days; and when they could not go out, turned them into the hold to stack the ship's stores into smaller compass, to make more room for the fish. The packed mass ran from the cabin partition to the sliding door behind the foc'sle stove; and Disko showed how there is great art in stowing cargo so as to bring a schooner to her best draft. The crew were thus kept lively till they recovered their spirits; and Harvey was tickled with a rope's end by Long Jack for being, as the Galway man said, "sorrowful as a sick cat over fwhat could n't be helped." He did a great deal of thinking in those weary days, and told Dan what he thought, and Dan agreed with him—even to the extent of asking for fried pies instead of hooking them.

But a week later the two nearly upset the the *Hattie S.* in a wild attempt to stab a shark with an old bayonet tied to a stick. The grim brute rubbed alongside the dory begging for small fish, and between the three of them it was a mercy they all got off alive.

At last, after playing blindman's-buff in the fog, there came a morning when Disko shouted down the foc'sle: "Hurry, boys! We 're in taown!"

# CHAPTER VIII

TO THE END of his days, Harvey will never forget that sight. The sun was just clear of the horizon they had not seen for nearly a week, and his low red light struck into the riding-sails of three fleets of anchored schooners—one to the north, one to the westward, and one to the south. There must have been nearly a hundred of them, of every possible make and build with, far away, a square-rigged Frenchman, all bowing and courtesying one to the other. From every boat dories were dropping away like bees from a crowded hive, and the clamour of voices, the rattling of ropes and blocks, and the splash of the oars carried for miles across the heaving water. The sails turned all colours, black, pearly-gray, and white, as the sun mounted; and more boats swung up through the mists to the southward.

The dories gathered in clusters, separated, reformed, and broke again, all heading one way; while men hailed and whistled and cat-called and sang, and the water was speckled with rubbish thrown overboard.

"It's a town," said Harvey. "Disko was right. It *is* a town!"

"I've seen smaller," said Disko. "There's about a thousand men here; an' yonder's the Virgin." he pointed to a vacant space of greenish sea, where there were no dories.

The *We're Here* skirted round the northern squadron, Disko waving his hand to friend after friend, and anchored as neatly as a racing yacht at the end of the season. The Bank fleet pass good seamanship in silence; but a bungler is jeered all along the line.

"Jest in time fer the caplin," cried the *Mary Chilton*.

"'Salt 'most wet?" asked the *King Philip*.

"Hey, Tom Platt! Come t' supper tonight?" said the *Henry Clay;* and so questions and answers flew back and forth. Men had met one another before, dory-fishing in the fog, and there is no place for gossip like the Bank fleet. They all seemed to know about Harvey's rescue, and asked if he were worth his salt yet. The young bloods jested with Dan,

101

who had a lively tongue of his own, and inquired after their
health by the town-nicknames they least liked. Manuel's
countrymen jabbered at him in their own language; and
even the silent cook was seen riding the jib-boom and shouting Gaelic to a friend as black as himself. After they had
buoyed the cable—all around the Virgin is rocky bottom,
and carelessness means chafed ground-tackle and danger
from drifting—after they had buoyed the cable, their dories
went forth to join the mob of boats anchored about a mile
away. The schooners rocked and dipped at a safe distance,
like mother ducks watching their brood, while the dories
behaved like mannerless ducklings.

As they drove into the confusion, boat banging boat, Harvey's ears tingled at the comments on his rowing. Every
dialect from Labrador to Long Island, with Portuguese, Nea-
politan, Lingua Franca, French, and Gaelic, with songs and
shoutings and new oaths, rattled round him, and he seemed
to be the butt of it all. For the first time in his life he felt
shy—perhaps that came from living so long with only the
*We're Heres*—among the scores of wild faces that rose and
fell with the reeling small craft. A gentle, breathing swell,
three furlongs from trough to barrel, would quietly shoulder
up a string of variously painted dories. They hung for an
instant, a wonderful frieze against the sky-line, and their
men pointed and hailed. Next moment the open mouths,
waving arms, and bare chests disappeared, while on another
swell came up an entirely new line of characters like paper
figures in a toy theatre. So Harvey stared. "Watch out!" said
Dan, flourishing a dip-net. "When I tell you dip, you dip.
The caplin 'll school any time from naow on. Where 'll we
lay, Tom Platt?"

Pushing, shoving, and hauling, greeting old friends here
and warning old enemies there, Commodore Tom Platt led
his little fleet well to leeward of the general crowd, and immediately three or four men began to haul on their anchors
with intent to lee-bow the *We're Heres*. But a yell of laughter went up as a dory shot from her station with exceeding
speed, its occupants pulling madly on the roding.

"Give her slack!" roared twenty voices. "Let him shake it
out."

"What 's the matter?" said Harvey, as the boat flashed
away to the southward. "He 's anchored, is n't he?"

"Anchored, sure enough, but his graound-tackle 's kinder shifty," said Dan, laughing. "Whale 's fouled it. . . . Dip, Harve! Here they come!"

The sea around them clouded and darkened, and then frizzed up in showers of tiny silver fish, and over a space of five or six acres the cod began to leap like trout in May; while behind the cod three or four broad gray-backs broke the water into boils.

Then everybody shouted and tried to haul up his anchor to get among the school, and fouled his neighbour's line and said what was in his heart, and dipped furiously with his dip-net, and shrieked cautions and advice to his companions, while the deep fizzed like freshly opened soda-water, and cod, men, and whales together flung in upon the luckless bait. Harvey was nearly knocked overboard by the handle of Dan's net. But in all the wild tumult he noticed, and never forgot, the wicked, set little eye—something like a circus elephant's eye—of a whale that drove along almost level with the water, and, so he said, winked at him. Three boats found their rodings fouled by these reckless mid-sea hunters, and were towed half a mile ere their horses shook the line free.

Then the caplin moved off, and five minutes later there was no sound except the splash of the sinkers overside, the flapping of the cod, and the whack of the muckles as the men stunned them. It was wonderful fishing. Harvey could see the glimmering cod below, swimming slowly in droves, biting as steadily as they swam. Bank law strictly forbids more than one hook on one line when the dories are on the Virgin or the Eastern Shoals; but so close lay the boats that even single hooks snarled, and Harvey found himself in hot argument with a gentle, hairy Newfoundlander on one side and a howling Portuguese on the other.

Worse than any tangle of fishing-lines was the confusion of the dory-rodings below water. Each man had anchored where it seemed good to him, drifting and rowing round his fixed point. As the fish struck on less quickly, each man wanted to haul up and get to better ground; but every third man found himself intimately connected with some four or five neighbours. To cut another's roding is crime unspeakable on the Banks; yet it was done, and done without detection, three or four times that day. Tom Platt caught a Maine

man in the black act and knocked him over the gunwale
with an oar, and Manuel served a fellow-countryman in the
same way. But Harvey's anchor-line was cut, and so was
Penn's, and they were turned into relief-boats to carry fish
to the *We 're Here* as the dories filled. The caplin schooled
once more at twilight, when the mad clamour was repeated;
and at dusk they rowed back to dress down by the light
of kerosene-lamps on the edge of the pen.

It was a huge pile, and they went to sleep while they were
dressing. Next day several boats fished right above the cap
of the Virgin; and Harvey, with them, looked down on the
very weed of that lonely rock, which rises to within twenty
feet of the surface. The cod were there in legions, marching
solemnly over the leathery kelp. When they bit, they bit all
together; and so when they stopped. There was a slack time
at noon, and the dories began to search for amusement. It
was Dan who sighted the *Hope of Prague* just coming up,
and as her boats joined the company they were greeted with
the question: "Who's the meanest man in the Fleet?"

Three hundred voices answered cheerily: "Nick Bra-ady."
It sounded like an organ chant.

"Who stole the lamp-wicks?" That was Dan's contribu-
tion.

"Nick Bra-ady," sang the boats.

"Who biled the salt bait fer soup?" This was an unknown
backbiter a quarter of a mile away.

Again the joyful chorus. Now, Brady was not especially
mean, but he had that reputation, and the Fleet made the
most of it. Then they discovered a man from a Truro boat
who, six years before, had been convicted of using a tackle
with five or six hooks—a "scrowger," they call it—on the
Shoals. Naturally, he had been christened "Scrowger Jim";
and though he had hidden himself on the Georges ever
since, he found his honours waiting for him full blown.
They took it up in a sort of firecracker chorus: "Jim! O Jim!
Jim! O Jim! Ssscrowger Jim!" That pleased everybody. And
when a poetical Beverly man—he had been making it up
all day, and talked about it for weeks—sang, "The *Carrie
Pitman's* anchor does n't hold her for a cent" the dories felt
that they were indeed fortunate. Then they had to ask that
Beverly man how he was off for beans, because even poets
must not have things all their own way. Every schooner and

"It was wonderful fishing. Harvey could see the glimmering cod below, . . . biting as steadily as they swam. . . . But so close lay the boats that even single hooks snarled."

nearly every man got it in turn. Was there a careless or dirty cook anywhere? The dories sang about him and his food. Was a schooner badly found? The Fleet was told at full length. Had a man hooked tobacco from a messmate? He was named in meeting; the name tossed from roller to roller. Disko's infallible judgments, Long Jack's market-boat that he had sold years ago, Dan's sweetheart (oh, but Dan was an angry boy!), Penn's bad luck with dory anchors, Salters' views on manure, Manuel's little slips from virtue ashore, and Harvey's ladylike handling of the oar—all were laid before the public; and as the fog fell around them in silvery sheets beneath the sun, the voices sounded like a bench of invisible judges pronouncing sentence.

The dories roved and fished and squabbled till a swell underran the sea. Then they drew more apart to save their sides, and some one called that if the swell continued the Virgin would break. A reckless Galway man with his nephew denied this, hauled up anchor, and rowed over the very rock itself. Many voices called them to come away, while others dared them to hold on. As the smooth-backed rollers passed to the southward, they hove the dory high and high into the mist, and dropped her in ugly, sucking, dimpled water, where she spun round her anchor, within a foot or two of the hidden rock. It was playing with death for mere bravado; and the boats looked on in uneasy silence till Long Jack rowed up behind his countrymen and quietly cut their roding.

"Can 't ye hear ut knockin'?" he cried. "Pull for your miserable lives! Pull!"

The men swore and tried to argue as the boat drifted; but the next swell checked a little, like a man tripping on a carpet. There was a deep sob and a gathering roar, and the Virgin flung up a couple of acres of foaming water, white, furious, and ghastly over the shoal sea. Then all the boats greatly applauded Long Jack, and the Galway men held their tongue.

"Ain't it elegant?" said Dan, bobbing like a young seal at home. "She 'll break about once every ha'af hour now, 'less the swell piles up good. What's her reg'lar time when she's at work, Tom Platt?"

"Once ivry fifteen minutes, to the tick. Harve, you 've

seen the greatest thing on the Banks; an' but for Long Jack you 'd seen some dead men too."

There came a sound of merriment where the fog lay thicker and the schooners were ringing their bells. A big bark nosed cautiously out of the mist, and was received with shouts and cries of, "Come along, darlin'," from the Irishry.

"Another Frenchman?" said Harvey.

"Hain't you eyes? She 's a Baltimore boat; goin' in fear an' tremblin'," said Dan. "We 'll guy the very sticks out of her. Guess it 's the fust time her skipper ever met up with the Fleet this way."

She was a black, buxom, eight-hundred-ton craft. Her mainsail was looped up, and her topsail flapped undecidedly in what little wind was moving. Now a bark is feminine beyond all other daughters of the sea, and this tall, hesitating creature, with her white and gilt figurehead, looked just like a bewildered woman half lifting her skirts to cross a muddy street under the jeers of bad little boys. That was very much her situation. She knew she was somewhere in the neighbourhood of the Virgin, had caught the roar of it, and was, therefore, asking her way. This is a small part of what she heard from the dancing dories:

"The Virgin? Fwhat are you talkin' of? This is Le Have on a Sunday mornin'. Go home an' sober up."

"Go home, ye tarrapin! Go home an' tell 'em we 're comin'."

Half a dozen voices together, in a most tuneful chorus, as her stern went down with a roll and a bubble into the troughs: "Thay-aah—she—strikes!"

"Hard up! Hard up fer your life! You 're on top of her now."

"Daown! Hard daown! Let go everything!"

"All hands to the pumps!"

"Daown jib an' pole her!"

Here the skipper lost his temper and said things. Instantly fishing was suspended to answer him, and he heard many curious facts about his boat and her next port of call. They asked him if he were insured; and whence he had stolen his anchor, because, they said, it belonged to the *Carrie Pitman;* they called his boat a mud-scow, and accused him of dumping garbage to frighten the fish; they offered to tow him and charge it to his wife; and one audacious youth slipped up almost under the counter, smacked it with his open palm, and yelled: "Gid up, Buck!"

The cook emptied a pan of ashes on him, and he replied with cod-heads. The bark's crew fired small coal from the galley, and the dories threatened to come aboard and "razee" her. They would have warned her at once had she been in real peril; but, seeing her well clear of the Virgin, they made the most of their chances. The fun was spoilt when the rock spoke again, a half-mile to windward, and the tormented bark set everything that would draw and went her ways; but the dories felt that the honours lay with them.

All that night the Virgin roared hoarsely; and next morning, over an angry, white-headed sea, Harvey saw the Fleet with flickering masts waiting for a lead. Not a dory was hove out till ten o'clock, when the two Jeraulds of the *Day's Eye,* imagining a lull which did not exist, set the example. In a minute half the boats were out and bobbing in the cockly swells, but Troop kept the *We 're Heres* at work dressing down. He saw no sense in "dares"; and as the storm grew that evening they had the pleasure of receiving wet strangers only too glad to make any refuge in the gale. The boys stood by the dory-tackles with lanterns, the men ready to haul, one eye cocked for the sweeping wave that would make them drop everything and hold on for dear life. Out of the dark would come a yell of "Dory! dory!" They would hook up and haul in a drenched man and a half-sunk boat, till their decks were littered down with nests of dories and the bunks were full. Five times in their watch did Harvey, with Dan, jump at the foregaff where it lay lashed on the boom, and cling with arms, legs, and teeth to rope and spar and sodden canvas as a big wave filled the decks. One dory was smashed to pieces, and the sea pitched the man head first on to the decks, cutting his forehead open; and about dawn, when the racing seas glimmered white all along their cold edges, another man, blue and ghastly, crawled in with a broken hand, asking news of his brother. Seven extra mouths sat down to breakfast: a Swede; a Chatham skipper; a boy from Hancock, Maine; one Duxbury, and three Provincetown men.

There was a general sorting out among the Fleet next day;

and though no one said anything, all ate with better appetites when boat after boat reported full crews aboard. Only a couple of Portuguese and an old man from Gloucester were drowned, but many were cut or bruised; and two schooners had parted their tackle and been blown to the southward, three days' sail. A man died on a Frenchman—it was the same bark that had traded tobacco with the *We 're Heres.* She slipped away quietly one wet, white morning, moved to a patch of deep water, her sails all hanging anyhow, and Harvey saw the funeral through Disko's spy-glass. It was only an oblong bundle slid overside. They did not seem to have any form of service, but in the night, at anchor, Harvey heard them across the star-powdered black water, singing something that sounded like a hymn. It went to a very slow tune.

> "La brigantine
> Qui va tourner,
> Roule et s'incline
> Pour m'entrainer.
>
>
> Oh, Vierge Marie
> Pour moi priez Dieu!
> Adieu, patrie;
> Québec, adieu!"

Tom Platt visited her, because, he said, the dead man was his brother as a Freemason. It came out that a wave had doubled the poor fellow over the heel of the bowsprit and broken his back. The news spread like a flash, for, contrary to general custom, the Frenchman held an auction of the dead man's kit,—he had no friends at St. Malo or Miquelon, —and everything was spread out on the top of the house, from his red knitted cap to the leather belt with the sheath-knife at the back. Dan and Harvey were out on twenty-fathom water in the *Hattie S.,* and naturally rowed over to join the crowd. It was a long pull, and they stayed some little time while Dan bought the knife, which had a curious brass handle. When they dropped overside and pushed off into a drizzle of rain and a lop of sea, it occurred to them that they might get into trouble for neglecting the lines.

"Guess 't won't hurt us any to be warmed up," said Dan, shivering under his oilskins, and they rowed on into the heart of a white fog, which, as usual, dropped on them without warning.

"There 's too much blame tide hereabouts to trust to your instinks," he said. "Heave over the anchor, Harve, and we 'll fish a piece till the thing lifts. Bend on your biggest lead. Three pound ain't any too much in this water. See how she 's tightened on her rodin' already."

There was quite a little bubble at the bows, where some irresponsible Bank current held the dory full stretch on her rope; but they could not see a boat's length in any direction. Harvey turned up his collar and bunched himself over his reel with the air of a wearied navigator. Fog had no special terrors for him now. They fished a while in silence, and found the cod struck on well. Then Dan drew the sheath-knife and tested the edge of it on the gunwale.

"That's a daisy," said Harvey. "How did you get it so cheap?"

"On account o' their blame Cath'lic superstitions," said Dan, jabbing with the bright blade. "They don't fancy takin' iron frum off a dead man, so to speak. 'See them Arichat Frenchmen step back when I bid?"

"But an auction ain't taking anything off a dead man. It's business."

"_We_ know it ain't, but there 's no goin' in the teeth o' superstition. That's one o' the advantages o' livin' in a progressive country." And Dan began whistling:

> "Oh Double Thatcher, how are you?
> Now Eastern Point comes inter view.
> The girls an' boys we soon shall see,
> At anchor off Cape Ann!"

"Why did n't that Eastport man bid, then? He bought his boots. Ain't Maine progressive?"

"Maine? Pshaw! They don't know enough, or they hain't got money enough, to paint their haouses in Maine. I 've seen 'em. The Eastport man he told me that the knife had been used—so the French captain told him—used up on the French coast last year."

"Cut a man? Heave 's the muckle." Harvey hauled in his fish, rebaited, and threw over.

"Killed him! Course, when I heard _that_ I was keener 'n ever to get it."

"Christmas! I did n't know it," said Harvey, turning round. "I'll give you a dollar for it when I—get my wages. Say, I 'll give you two dollars."

"Honest? D' you like it as much as all that?" said Dan, flushing. "Well, to tell the truth, I kinder got it for you—to give; but I did n't let on till I saw how you 'd take it. It 's yours and welcome, Harve, because we 're dory-mates, and so on and so forth, an' so followin'. Catch a-holt!"

He held it out, belt and all.

"But look at here. Dan, I don't see——"

"Take it. 'T ain't no use to me. I wish you to hev it."

The temptation was irresistible. "Dan, you're a white man," said Harvey. "I 'll keep it as long as I live."

"That 's good hearin'," said Dan, with a pleasant laugh; and then, anxious to change the subject: " 'Look 's if your line was fast to somethin'."

"Fouled, I guess," said Harve, tugging. Before he pulled up he fastened the belt round him, and with deep delight heard the tip of the sheath click on the thwart. "Concern the thing!" he cried. "She acts as though she were on strawberry-bottom. It 's all sand here, ain't it?"

Dan reached over and gave a judgmatic tweak. "Holibut 'll act that way 'f he 's sulky. Thet 's no strawberrybottom. Yank her once or twice. She gives, sure. Guess we 'd better haul up an' make certain."

They pulled together, making fast at each turn on the cleats, and the hidden weight rose sluggishly.

"Prize, oh! Haul!" shouted Dan, but the shout ended in a shrill, double shriek of horror, for out of the sea came—the body of the dead Frenchman buried two days before! The hook had caught him under the right armpit, and he swayed, erect and horrible, head and shoulders above water. His arms were tied to his side, and—he had no face. The boys fell over each other in a heap at the bottom of the dory, and there they lay while the thing bobbed alongside, held on the shortened line.

"The tide—the tide brought him!" said Harvey with quivering lips, as he fumbled at the clasp of the belt.

"Oh, Lord! Oh, Harve!" groaned Dan, "be quick. He 's come for it. Let him have it. Take it off."

"I don't want it! I don't want it!" cried Harvey. "I can't find the bu-buckle."

"Quick, Harve! He 's on your line!"

Harvey sat up to unfasten the belt, facing the head that had no face under its streaming hair. "He 's fast still," he whispered to Dan, who slipped out his knife and cut the line, as Harvey flung the belt far overside. The body shot down with a plop, and Dan cautiously rose to his knees, whiter than the fog.

"He come for it. He come for it. I 've seen a stale one hauled up on a trawl and I did n't much care, but *he* come to us special."

"I wish—I wish I had n't taken the knife. Then he 'd have come on *your* line."

"Dunno as thet would ha' made any differ. We 're both scared out o' ten years' growth. Oh, Harve, did ye see his head?"

"Did I? I 'll never forget it. But look at here, Dan; it could n't have been *meant*. It was only the tide."

"Tide! He come for it, Harve. Why, they sunk him six miles to south'ard o' the Fleet, an' we 're two miles from where he 's lyin' now. They told me he was weighted with a fathom an' a half o' chain-cable."

" 'Wonder what he did with the knife—up on the French coast?"

"Something bad. 'Guess he 's bound to take it with him to the Judgment, an' so—— What are you doin' with the fish?"

"Heaving 'em overboard," said Harvey.

"What for? *We* sha'n't eat 'em."

"I don't care. I had to look at his face while I was takin' the belt off. You can keep your catch if you like. I 've no use for mine."

Dan said nothing, but threw his fish over again.

"Guess it 's best to be on the safe side," he murmured at last. "I 'd give a month's pay if this fog 'u 'd lift. Things go abaout in a fog that ye don't see in clear weather— yo-hoes an' hollerers and such like. I 'm sorter relieved he come the way he did instid o' walkin'. He might ha' walked."

"Do-on't, Dan! We 're right on top of him now. 'Wish I was safe aboard, bein' pounded by Uncle Salters."

"They 'll be lookin' fer us in a little. Gimme the tooter." Dan took the tin dinner-horn, but paused before he blew.

"Go on," said Harvey. "I don't want to stay here all night."

"Question is, haow *he'd* take it. There was a man frum down the coast told me once he was in a schooner where they darse n't ever blow a horn to the dories, becaze the skipper—not the man he was with, but a captain that had run her five years before—he' d drownded a boy alongside in a drunk fit; an' ever after, that boy he'd row alongside too and shout, 'Dory! dory!' with the rest."

"Dory! Dory!" a muffled voice cried through the fog. They cowered again, and the horn dropped from Dan's hand.

"Hold on!" cried Harvey; "it 's the cook."

"Dunno what made me think o' thet fool tale, either," said Dan. "It 's the doctor, sure enough."

"Dan! Danny! Oooh, Dan! Harve! Harvey! Oooh, Haarveee!"

"We 're here," sung both boys together. They heard oars, but could see nothing till the cook, shining and dripping, rowed into them.

"What iss happened?" said he. "You will be beaten at home."

"Thet 's what we want. Thet 's what we 're sufferin' for," said Dan. "Anything homey 's good enough fer us. We 've had kinder depressin' company." As the cook passed them a line, Dan told him the tale.

"Yess! He come for hiss knife," was all he said at the end.

Never had the little rocking *We 're Here* looked so deliciously home-like as when the cook, born and bred in fogs, rowed them back to her. There was a warm glow of light from the cabin and a satisfying smell of food forward, and it was heavenly to hear Disko and the others, all quite alive and solid, leaning over the rail and promising them a first-class pounding. But the cook was a black master of strategy. He did not get the dories aboard till he had given the more striking points of the tale, explaining as he backed and bumped round the counter how Harvey was the mascot to destroy any possible bad luck. So the boys came overside as rather uncanny heroes, and every one asked them questions instead of pounding them for making trouble. Little Penn delivered quite a speech on the folly of superstitions; but public opinion was against him and in favour of Long Jack, who told the most excruciating ghost-stories, till nearly midnight. Under that influence no one except Salters and Penn said anything about "idolatry," when the cook put a lighted candle, a cake of flour and water, and a pinch of salt on a shingle, and floated them out astern to keep the Frenchman quiet in case he was still restless. Dan lit the candle because he had bought the belt, and the cook grunted and muttered charms as long as he could see the ducking point of flame.

Said Harvey to Dan, as they turned in after watch: "How about progress and Catholic superstitions?"

"Huh! I guess I 'm as enlightened and progressive as the next man, but when it comes to a dead St. Malo deck-hand scarin' a couple o' pore boys stiff fer the sake of a thirty-cent knife, why, then, the cook can take hold fer all o' me. I mistrust furriners, livin' or dead."

Next morning all, except the cook, were rather ashamed of the ceremonies, and went to work double tides, speaking gruffly to one another.

The *We 're Here* was racing neck and neck for her last few loads against the *Parry Norman;* and so close was the struggle that the Fleet took side and betted tobacco. All hands worked at the lines or dressing-down till they fell asleep where they stood—beginning before dawn and ending when it was too dark to see. They even used the cook as pitcher, and turned Harvey into the hold to pass salt, while Dan helped to dress down. Luckily a *Parry Norman* man sprained his ankle falling down the foc'sle, and the *We 're Heres* gained. Harvey could not see how one more fish could be crammed into her, but Disko and Tom Platt stowed and stowed, and planked the mass down with big stones from the ballast, and there was always "jest another day's work." Disko did not tell them when all the salt was wetted. He rolled to the lazarette aft the cabin and began hauling out the big mainsail. This was at ten in the morning. The riding-sail was down and the main- and topsail were up by noon, and dories came alongside with letters for home, envying their good fortune. At last she cleared decks, hoisted her flag,—as is the right of the first boat off the Banks,—up-anchored, and began to move. Disko pretended that he wished to accommodate folk who had not

sent in their mail, and so worked her gracefully in and out
among the schooners. In reality, that was his little triumphant procession, and for the fifth year running it
showed what kind of mariner he was. Dan's accordion and
Tom Platt's fiddle supplied the music of the magic verse
you must not sing till all the salt is wet:

"Hih! Yih! Yoho! Send your letters raound!
All our salt is wetted, an' the anchor's off the graound!
Bend, oh, bend your mains'l, we're back to Yankeeland—
            With fifteen hunder' quintal,
            An' fifteen hunder' quintal,
            'Teen hunder' toppin' quintal,
'Twix old 'Queereau an' Grand."

The last letters pitched on deck wrapped round pieces
of coal, and the Gloucester men shouted messages to their
wives and women-folks and owners, while the *We 're
Here* finished the musical ride through the Fleet, her head-
sails quivering like a man's hand when he raises it to say
good-by.

Harvey very soon discovered that the *We 're Here,* with
her riding-sail, strolling from berth to berth, and the *We 're
Here* headed west by south under home canvas, were two
very different boats. There was a bite and kick to the wheel
even in "boy's" weather; he could feel the dead weight in
the hold flung forward mightily across the surges, and the
streaming line of bubbles overside made his eyes dizzy.

Disko kept them busy fiddling with the sails; and when
those were flattened like a racing yacht's, Dan had to wait
on the big topsail, which was put over by hand every time
she went about. In spare moments they pumped, for the
packed fish dripped brine, which does not improve a cargo.
But since there was no fishing, Harvey had time to look
at the sea from another point of view. The low-sided
schooner was naturally on most intimate terms with her
surroundings. They saw little of the horizon save when she
topped a swell; and usually she was elbowing, fidgeting,
and coaxing her steadfast way through gray, gray-blue, or
black hollows laced across and across with streaks of shivering foam; or rubbing herself caressingly along the flank
of some bigger water-hill. It was as if she said: "You

Dressing down on the "We're Here."

would n't hurt me, surely? I 'm only the little *We 're Here*."
Then she would slide away chuckling softly to herself till
she was brought up by some fresh obstacle. The dullest of
folk cannot see this kind of thing hour after hour through
long days without noticing it; and Harvey, being anything
but dull, began to comprehend and enjoy the dry chorus
of wave-tops turning over with a sound of incessant tearing; the hurry of the winds working across open spaces and
herding the purple-blue cloud-shadows; the splendid up-
heaval of the red sunrise; the folding and packing away of
the morning mists, wall after wall withdrawn across the
white floors; the salty glare and blaze of noon; the kiss of
rain falling over thousands of dead, flat square miles; the
chilly blackening of everything at the day's end; and
the million wrinkles of the sea under the moonlight, when
the jib-boom solemnly poked at the low stars, and Harvey
went down to get a doughnut from the cook.

But the best fun was when the boys were put on the
wheel together, Tom Platt within hail, and she cuddled her
lee-rail down to the crashing blue, and kept a little homemade rainbow arching unbroken over her windlass. Then
the jaws of the booms whined against the masts, and the
sheets creaked, and the sails filled with roaring; and when
she slid into a hollow she trampled like a woman tripped
in her own silk dress, and came out, her jib wet half-way
up, yearning and peering for the tall twin-lights of
Thatcher's Island.

They left the cold gray of the Bank sea, saw the lum-
ber-ships making for Quebec by the Straits of St. Law-
rence, with the Jersey salt-brigs from Spain and Sicily;
found a friendly northeaster off Artimon Bank that drove
them within view of the East light of Sable Island,—a
sight Disko did not linger over,—and stayed with them
past Western and Le Have, to the northern fringe of
Georges. From there they picked up the deeper water, and
let her go merrily.

"Hattie 's pulling on the string," Dan confided to Harvey. "Hattie an' Ma. Next Sunday you 'll be hirin' a boy
to throw water on the windows to make ye go to sleep.
'Guess you 'll keep with us till your folks come. Do you
know the best of gettin' ashore again?"

"Hot bath?" said Harvey. His eyebrows were all white with dried spray.

"That 's good, but a night-shirt 's better. I 've been dreamin' o' night-shirts ever since we bent our mainsail. Ye can wiggle your toes then. Ma 'll hev a new one fer me, all washed soft. It 's home, Harve. It 's home! Ye can sense it in the air. We 're runnin' into the aidge of a hot wave naow, an' I can smell the bayberries. Wonder if we 'll get in fer supper. Port a trifle."

The hesitating sails flapped and lurched in the close air as the deep smoothed out, blue and oily, round them. When they whistled for a wind only the rain came in spiky rods, bubbling and drumming, and behind the rain the thunder and the lighning of mid-August. They lay on the deck with bare feet and arms, telling one another what they would order at their first meal ashore; for now the land was in plain sight. A Gloucester swordfish-boat drifted alongside, a man in the little pulpit on the bowsprit flourished his harpoon, his bare head plastered down with the wet. "And all 's well!" he sang cheerily, as though he were watch on a big liner. "Wouverman 's waiting fer you, Disko. What 's the news o' the Fleet?"

Disko shouted it and passed on, while the wild summer storm pounded overhead and the lightning flickered along the capes from four different quarters at once. It gave the low circle of hills round Gloucester Harbor, Ten Pound Island, the fish-sheds, with the broken line of house-roofs, and each spar and buoy on the water, in blinding photographs that came and went a dozen times to the minute as the *We 're Here* crawled in on half-flood, and the whistling-buoy moaned and mourned behind her. Then the storm died out in long, separated, vicious dags of blue-white flame, followed by a single roar like the roar of a mortar-battery, and the shaken air tingled under the stars as it got back to silence.

"The flag, the flag!" said Disko, suddenly, pointing upward.

"What is ut?" said Long Jack.

"Otto! Ha'af mast. They can see us frum shore now."

"I 'd clean forgot. He 's no folk to Gloucester, has he?"

"Girl he was goin' to be married to this fall."

"Mary pity her!" said Long Jack, and lowered the little

"Dories came alongside with letters for home."

flag half-mast for the sake of Otto, swept overboard in a gale off Le Have three months before.

Disko wiped the wet from his eyes and led the *We 're Here* to Wouverman's wharf, giving his orders in whispers, while she swung round moored tugs and night-watchmen hailed her from the ends of inky-black piers. Over and above the darkness and the mystery of the procession, Harvey could feel the land close round him once more, with all its thousands of people asleep, and the smell of earth after rain, and the familiar noise of a switching-engine coughing to herself in a freight-yard; and all those things made his heart beat and his throat dry up as he stood by the foresheet. They heard the anchor-watch snoring on a lighthouse-tug, nosed into a pocket of darkness where a lantern glimmered on either side; somebody waked with a grunt, threw them a rope, and they made fast to a silent wharf flanked with great iron-roofed sheds full of warm emptiness, and lay there without a sound.

Then Harvey sat down by the wheel, and sobbed and sobbed as though his heart would break, and a tall woman who had been sitting on a weigh-scale dropped down into the schooner and kissed Dan once on the cheek; for she was his mother, and she had seen the *We 're Here* by the lightning flashes. She took no notice of Harvey till he had recovered himself a little and Disko had told her his story. Then they went to Disko's house together as the dawn was breaking; and until the telegraph office was open and he could wire his folk, Harvey Cheyne was perhaps the loneliest boy in all America. But the curious thing was that Disko and Dan seemed to think none the worse of him for crying.

Wouverman was not ready for Disko's prices till Disko, sure that the *We 're Here* was at least a week ahead of any other Gloucester boat, had given him a few days to swallow them; so all hands played about the streets, and Long Jack stopped the Rocky Neck trolley, on principle, as he said, till the conductor let him ride free. But Dan went about with his freckled nose in the air, bung-full of mystery and most haughty to his family.

"Dan, I 'll hev to lay inter you ef you act this way," said

Troop, pensively. "Sence we 've come ashore this time you 've bin a heap too fresh."

"I 'd lay into him naow ef he was mine," said Uncle Salters, sourly. He and Penn boarded with the Troops.

"Oho!" said Dan, shuffling with the accordion round the backyard, ready to leap the fence if the enemy advanced. "Dan, you 're welcome to your own judgment, but remember I 've warned ye. Your own flesh an' blood ha' warned ye! 'T ain't any o' *my* fault ef you 're mistook, but I 'll be on deck to watch ye. An' ez fer *yeou*, Uncle Salters, Pharaoh's chief butler ain't in it 'longside o' you! You watch aout an' wait. You 'll be plowed under like your own blamed clover; but me—Dan Troop—I 'll flourish like a green bay-tree because *I* war n't stuck on my own opinion."

Disko was smoking in all his shore dignity and a pair of beautiful carpet-slippers. "You 're gettin' ez crazy as poor Harve. You two go araound gigglin' an' squinchin' an' kickin' each other under the table till there 's no peace in the haouse," said he.

"There 's goin' to be a heap less—fer some folks," Dan replied. "You wait an' see."

He and Harvey went out on the trolley to East Glouces-ter, where they tramped through the bayberry bushes to the lighthouse, and lay down on the big red boulders and laughed themselves hungry. Harvey had shown Dan a tele-gram, and the two swore to keep silence till the shell burst.

"Harve's folk?" said Dan, with an unruffled face after supper. "Well, I guess they don't amount to much of any-thing, or we 'd ha' heard frum 'em by naow. His pop keeps a kind o' store out West. Maybe he 'll give you 's much as five dollars, Dad."

"What did I tell ye?" said Salters. "Don't sputter over your vittles, Dan."

# CHAPTER IX

WHATEVER HIS private sorrows may be, a multimillionaire, like any other workingman, should keep abreast of his business. Harvey Cheyne, senior, had gone East late in June to meet a woman broken down, half mad, who dreamed day and night of her son drowning in the gray seas. He had surrounded her with doctors, trained nurses, massage-women, and even faith-cure companions, but they were useless. Mrs. Cheyne lay still and moaned, or talked of her boy by the hour together to any one who would listen. Hope she had none, and who could offer it? All she needed was assurance that drowning did not hurt; and her husband watched to guard lest she should make the experiment. Of his own sorrow he spoke little—hardly realized the depth of it till he caught himself asking the calendar on his writing-desk, "What's the use of going on?"

There had always lain a pleasant notion at the back of his head that, some day, when he had rounded off everything and the boy had left college, he would take his son to his heart and lead him into his possessions. Then that boy, he argued, as busy fathers do, would instantly become his companion, partner, and ally, and there would follow splendid years of great works carried out together—the old head backing the young fire. Now his boy was dead—lost at sea, as it might have been a Swede sailor from one of Cheyne's big tea-ships; the wife dying, or worse; he himself was trodden down by platoons of women and doctors and maids and attendants; worried almost beyond endurance by the shift and change of her poor restless whims; hopeless, with no heart to meet his many enemies.

He had taken the wife to his raw new palace in San Diego, where she and her people occupied a wing of great price, and Cheyne, in a veranda-room, between a secretary and a typewriter, who was also a telegraphist, toiled along wearily from day to day. There was a war of rates among four Western railroads in which he was supposed to be interested; a devastating strike had developed in his lumber camps in Oregon, and the legislature of the State of California, which has no love for its makers, was preparing open war against him.

Ordinarily he would have accepted battle ere it was offered, and have waged a pleasant and unscrupulous campaign. But now he sat limply, his soft black hat pushed forward on to his nose, his big body shrunk inside his loose clothes, staring at his boots or the Chinese junks in the bay, and assenting absently to the secretary's questions as he opened the Saturday mail.

Cheyne was wondering how much it would cost to drop everything and pull out. He carried huge insurances, could buy himself royal annuities, and between one of his places in Colorado and a little society (that would do the wife good), say in Washington and the South Carolina islands, a man might forget plans that had come to nothing. On the other hand . . .

The click of the typewriter stopped; the girl was looking at the secretary who had turned white.

He passed Cheyne a telegram repeated from San Francisco:

*Picked up by fishing schooner We're Here having fallen off boat great times on Banks fishing all well waiting Gloucester Mass care Disko Troop for money or orders wire what shall do and how is Mama Harvey N. Cheyne.*

The father let it fall, laid his head down on the rollertop of the shut desk, and breathed heavily. The secretary ran for Mrs. Cheyne's doctor who found Cheyne pacing to and fro.

"What—what d 'you think of it? Is it possible? Is there any meaning to it? I can 't quite make it out," he cried.

"I can," said the doctor. "I lose seven thousand a year —that 's all." He thought of the struggling New York practice he had dropped at Cheyne's imperious bidding, and returned the telegram with a sigh.

"You mean you 'd tell her? 'May be a fraud?"

"What 's the motive?" said the doctor coolly. "Detection 's too certain. It 's the boy sure enough."

Enter a French maid, impudently, as an indispensable one who is kept on only by large wages.

"Mrs. Cheyne she say you must come at once. She think you are seek."

The master of thirty millions bowed his head meekly and followed Suzanne; and a thin, high voice on the upper landing of the great white-wood square staircase cried: "What is it? What has happened?"

No door could keep out the shriek that rang through the echoing house a moment later, when her husband blurted out the news.

"And that 's all right," said the doctor, serenely, to the typewriter. "About the only medical statement in novels with any truth to it is that joy don't kill, Miss Kinzey."

"I know it; but we 've a heap to do first." Miss Kinzey was from Milwaukee, somewhat direct of speech; and as her fancy leaned towards the secretary, she divined there was work in hand. He was looking earnestly at the vast roller-map of America on the wall.

"Milsom, we 're going right across. Private car—straight through—Boston. Fix the connections," shouted Cheyne down the staircase.

"I thought so."

The secretary turned to the typewriter, and their eyes met (out of that was born a story—nothing to do with this story). She looked inquiringly, doubtful of his resources. He signed to her to move to the Morse as a general brings brigades into action. Then he swept his hand musician-wise through his hair, regarded the ceiling, and set to work, while Miss Kinzey's white fingers called up the Continent of America.

"*K. H. Wade, Los Angeles*—— The 'Constance' is at Los Angeles, is n't she, Miss Kinzey?"

"Yep." Miss Kinzey nodded between clicks as the secretary looked at his watch.

"Ready? *Send 'Constance,' private car, here, and arrange for special to leave here Sunday in time to connect with New York Limited at Sixteenth Street, Chicago, Tuesday next.*"

Click—click—click! "Could n't you better that?"

"Not on those grades. That gives 'em sixty hours from here to Chicago. They won't gain anything by taking a special east of that. Ready? *Also arrange with Lake Shore and Michigan Southern to take 'Constance' on New York*

*Central and Hudson River Buffalo to Albany, and B. and
A. the same Albany to Boston. Indispensable I should
reach Boston Wednesday evening. Be sure nothing pre-
vents. Have also wired Canniff, Toucey, and Barnes.—*
Sign, Cheyne."

Miss Kinzey nodded, and the secretary went on.

"Now then, Canniff, Toucey, and Barnes, of course.
Ready? *Canniff, Chicago. Please take my private car 'Constance' from Santa Fé at Sixteenth Street next Tuesday
p. m. on N. Y. Limited through to Buffalo and deliver
N. Y. C. for Albany.*—Ever bin to N' York, Miss Kinzey?
We'll go some day.—Ready? *Take car Buffalo to Albany
on Limited Tuesday p. m.* That's for Toucey."

"Have n't bin to Noo York, but I know *that!*" with a
toss of the head.

"Beg pardon. Now, Boston and Albany, Barnes, same
instructions from Albany through to Boston. Leave three-
five p.m. (you need n't wire that); arrive nine-five p.m.
Wednesday. That covers everything Wade will do, but
it pays to shake up the managers."

"It 's great," said Miss Kinzey, with a look of admira-
tion. This was the kind of man she understood and ap-
preciated.

" 'T is n't bad," said Milsom, modestly. "Now, any one
but me would have lost thirty hours and spent a week
working out the run, instead of handing him over to the
Santa Fé straight to Chicago."

"But see here, about that Noo York Limited. Chauncey Depew himself could n't hitch his car to *her,*" Miss
Kinzey suggested, recovering herself.

"Yes, but this is n't Chauncey. It 's Cheyne—lightning.
It goes."

"Even so. Guess we 'd better wire the boy. You 've forgotten that, anyhow."

"I 'll ask."

When he returned with the father's message bidding
Harvey to meet them in Boston at an appointed hour,
he found Miss Kinzey laughing over the keys. Then Milsom laughed too, for the frantic clicks from Los Angeles
ran: *"We want to know why—why—why? General un-
easiness developed and spreading."*

Ten minutes later Chicago appealed to Miss Kinzey in

these words: *"If crime of century is maturing please warn friends in time. We are getting to cover here."*

This was capped by a message from Topeka (and wherein Topeka was concerned even Milsom could not guess): *"Don't shoot, Colonel. We'll come down."*

Cheyne smiled grimly at the consternation of his enemies when the telegrams were laid before him. "They think we're on the warpath. Tell 'em we don't feel like fighting just now, Milsom. Tell 'em what we're going for. I guess you and Miss Kinzey had better come along, though it is n't likely I shall do any business on the road. Tell 'em the truth—for once."

So the truth was told. Miss Kinzey clicked in the sentiment while the secretary added the memorable quotation, "Let us have peace," and in board rooms two thousand miles away the representatives of sixty-three million dollars' worth of variously manipulated railroad interests breathed more freely. Cheyne was flying to meet the only son, so miraculously restored to him. The bear was seeking his cub, not the bulls. Hard men who had their knives drawn to fight for their financial lives put away the weapons and wished him God-speed, while half a dozen panic-smitten tin-pot roads perked up their heads and spoke of the wonderful things they would have done had not Cheyne buried the hatchet.

It was a busy week-end, among the wires; for now that their anxiety was removed, men and cities hastened to accommodate. Los Angeles called to San Diego and Barstow that the Southern California engineers might know and be ready in their lonely round-houses; Barstow passed the word to the Atlantic and Pacific; and Albuquerque flung it the whole length of the Atchison, Topeka, and Santa Fé management, even into Chicago. An engine combination-car with crew, and the great and gilded "Constance" private car were to be "expedited" over those two thousand three hundred and fifty miles. The train would take precedence of one hundred and seventy-seven others meeting and passing; dispatchers and crews of every one of those said trains must be notified. Sixteen locomotives, sixteen engineers, and sixteen firemen would be needed—each and every one the best available. Two and one half minutes would be allowed for changing en-

gines, three for watering, and two for coaling. "Warn the
men, and arrange tanks and chutes accordingly: for Harvey Cheyne is in a hurry, a hurry—a hurry," sang the
wires. "Forty miles an hour will be expected, and division
superintendents will accompany this special over their re-
spective divisions. From San Diego to Sixteenth Street,
Chicago, let the magic carpet be laid down. Hurry! Oh,
hurry!"

"It will be hot," said Cheyne, as they rolled out of San
Diego in the dawn of Sunday. "We 're going to hurry,
Mama, just as fast as ever we can; but I really don't think
there 's any good of your putting on your bonnet and
gloves yet. You 'd much better lie down and take your
medicine. I 'd play you a game of dominoes, but it 's
Sunday."

"I'll be good. Oh, I *will* be good. Only—taking off my
bonnet makes me feel as if we 'd never get there."

"Try to sleep a little, Mama, and we 'll be in Chicago
before you know."

"But it 's Boston, Father. Tell them to hurry."

The six-foot drivers were hammering their way to San
Bernardino and the Mohave wastes, but this was no
grade for speed. That would come later. The heat of the
desert followed the heat of the hills as they turned east
to the Needles and the Colorado River. The car cracked
in the utter drouth and glare, and they put crushed ice to
Mrs. Cheyne's neck, and toiled up the long, long grades,
past Ash Fork, towards Flagstaff, where the forests and
quarries are, under the dry remote skies. The needle of
the speed-indicator flicked and wagged to and fro; the
cinders rattled on the roof, and a whirl of dust sucked
after the whirling wheels. The crew of the combination
sat on their bunks, panting in their shirt-sleeves, and
Cheyne found himself among them shouting old, old
stories of the railroad that every trainman knows, above
the roar of the car. He told them about his son, and how
the sea had given up its dead, and they nodded and spat
and rejoiced with him; asked after "her, back there," and
whether she could stand it if the engineer "let her out a
piece," and Cheyne thought she could. Accordingly, the
great fire-horse was "let-out" from Flagstaff to Winslow,
till a division superintendent protested.

But Mrs. Cheyne, in the boudoir stateroom, where the French maid, sallow-white with fear, clung to the silver door-handle, only moaned a little and begged her husband to bid them "hurry." And so they dropped the dry sands and moon-struck rocks of Arizona behind them, and grilled on till the crash of the couplings and the wheeze of the brake-hose told them they were at Coolidge by the Continental Divide.

Three bold and experienced men—cool, confident, and dry when they began; white, quivering, and wet when they finished their trick at those terrible wheels—swung her over the great lift from Albuquerque to Glorietta and beyond Springer, up and up to the Raton Tunnel on the State line, whence they dropped rocking into La Junta, had sight of the Arkansas, and tore down the long slope to Dodge City, where Cheyne took comfort once again from setting his watch an hour ahead.

There was very little talk in the car. The secretary and typewriter sat together on the stamped Spanish-leather cushions by the plate-glass observation-window at the rear end, watching the surge and ripple of the ties crowded back behind them, and, it is believed, making notes of the scenery. Cheyne moved nervously between his own extravagant gorgeousness and the naked necessity of the combination, an unlit cigar in his teeth, till the pitying crews forgot that he was their tribal enemy, and did their best to entertain him.

At night the bunched electrics lit up that distressful palace of all the luxuries, and they fared sumptuously, swinging on through the emptiness of abject desolation. Now they heard the swish of a water-tank, and the guttural voice of a Chinaman, the clink-clink of hammers that tested the Krupp steel wheels, and the oath of a tramp chased off the rear-platform; now the solid crash of coal shot into the tender; and now a beating back of noises as they flew past a waiting train. Now they looked out into great abysses, a trestle purring beneath their tread, or up to rocks that barred out half the stars. Now scaur and ravine changed and rolled back to jagged mountains on the horizon's edge, and now broke into hills lower and lower, till at last came the true plains.

At Dodge City an unknown hand threw in a copy of

a Kansas paper containing some sort of an interview with Harvey, who had evidently fallen in with an enterprising reporter, telegraphed on from Boston. The joyful journalese revealed that it was beyond question their boy, and it soothed Mrs. Cheyne for a while. Her one word "hurry" was conveyed by the crews to the engineers at Nickerson, Topeka, and Marceline, where the grades are easy, and they brushed the Continent behind them. Towns and villages were close together now, and a man could feel here that he moved among people.

"I can't see the dial, and my eyes ache so. What are we doing?"

"The very best we can, Mama. There 's no sense in getting in before the Limited. We 'd only have to wait."

"I don't care. I want to feel we 're moving. Sit down and tell me the miles."

Cheyne sat down and read the dial for her (there were some miles which stand for records to this day), but the seventy-foot car never changed its long steamer-like roll, moving through the heat with the hum of a giant bee. Yet the speed was not enough for Mrs. Cheyne; and the heat, the remorseless August heat, was making her giddy; the clock-hands would not move, and when, oh, when would they be in Chicago?

It is not true that, as they changed engines at Fort Madison, Cheyne passed over to the Amalgamated Brotherhood of Locomotive Engineers an endowment sufficient to enable them to fight him and his fellows on equal terms for evermore. He paid his obligations to engineers and firemen as he believed they deserved, and only his bank knows what he gave the crews who had sympathized with him. It is on record that the last crew took entire charge of switching operations at Sixteenth Street, because "she" was in a doze at last, and Heaven was to help any one who bumped her.

Now the highly paid specialist who conveys the Lake Shore and Michigan Southern Limited from Chicago to Elkhart is something of an autocrat, and he does not approve of being told how to back up to a car. None the less he handled the "Constance" as if she might have been a load of dynamite, and when the crew rebuked him, they did it in whispers and dumb show.

"Pshaw!" said the Atchison, Topeka, and Santa Fé men, discussing life later, "we were n't runnin' for a record. Harvey Cheyne's wife, she were sick back, an' we didn't want to jounce her. Come to think of it, our runnin' time from San Diego to Chicago was 57.54. You can tell that to them Eastern way-trains. When we 're tryin' for a record, we 'll let you know."

To the Western man (though this would not please either city) Chicago and Boston are cheek by jowl, and some railroads encourage the delusion. The Limited whirled the "Constance" into Buffalo and the arms of the New York Central and Hudson River (illustrious magnates with white whiskers and gold charms on their watch-chains boarded her here to talk a little business to Cheyne), who slid her gracefully into Albany, where the Boston and Albany completed the run from tide-water to tide-water—total time, eighty-seven hours and thirty-five minutes, or three days, fifteen hours and one half. Harvey was waiting for them.

AFTER violent emotion most people and all boys demand food. They feasted the returned prodigal behind drawn curtains, cut off in their great happiness, while the trains roared in and out around them. Harvey ate, drank, and enlarged on his adventures all in one breath, and when he had a hand free his mother fondled it. His voice was thickened with living in the open, salt air; his palms were rough and hard, his wrists dotted with marks of gurry-sores; and a fine full flavour of cod-fish hung round rubber boots and blue jersey.

The father, well used to judging men, looked at him keenly. He did not know what enduring harm the boy might have taken. Indeed, he caught himself thinking that he knew very little whatever of his son; but he distinctly remembered an unsatisfied, dough-faced youth who took delight in "calling down the old man," and reducing his mother to tears—such a person as adds to the gaiety of public rooms and hotel piazzas, where the ingenuous young of the wealthy play with or revile the bell-boys. But this well set-up fisher-youth did not wriggle, looked at him with eyes steady, clear, and unflinching, and spoke in a tone distinctly, even startlingly, respectful. There was that in his

voice, too, which seemed to promise that the change might
be permanent, and that the new Harvey had come to stay.

"Some one 's been coercing him," thought Cheyne. "Now
Constance would never have allowed that. Don't see as
Europe could have done it any better."

"But why did n't you tell this man, Troop, who you
were?" the mother repeated, when Harvey had expanded his
story at least twice.

"Disko Troop, dear. The best man that ever walked a
deck. I don't care who the next is."

"Why did n't you tell him to put you ashore? You know
Papa would have made it up to him ten times over."

"I know it; but he thought I was crazy. I 'm afraid I
called him a thief because I could n't find the bills in my
pocket."

"A sailor found them by the flagstaff that—that night,"
sobbed Mrs. Cheyne.

"That explains it, then. I don't blame Troop any. I just
said I would n't work—on a Banker, too—and of course
he hit me on the nose, and oh! I bled like a stuck hog."

"My poor darling! They must have abused you horribly."

"Dunno quite. Well, after that, I saw a light."

Cheyne slapped his leg and chuckled. This was going
to be a boy after his own hungry heart. He had never seen
precisely that twinkle in Harvey's eye before.

"And the old man gave me ten and a half a month; he 's
paid me half now; and I took hold with Dan and pitched
right in. I can't do a man's work yet. But I can handle a dory
'most as well as Dan, and I don't get rattled in a fog—
much; and I can take my trick in light winds—that 's steer-
ing, dear—and I can 'most bait up a trawl, and I know my
ropes, of course; and I can pitch fish till the cows come home,
and I 'm great on old Josephus, and I 'll show you how I
can clear coffee with a piece of fish-skin, and—I think I 'll
have another cup, please. Say, you 've no notion what a heap
of work there is in ten and a half a month!"

"I began with eight and a half, my son," said Cheyne.

" 'That so? You never told me, sir."

"You never asked, Harve. I 'll tell you about it some day,
if you care to listen. Try a stuffed olive."

"Troop says *the* most interesting thing in the world is

to find out how the next man gets his vittles. It 's great to have a trimmed-up meal again. We were well fed, though. But mug on the Banks. Disko fed us first-class. He 's a great man. And Dan—that 's his son—Dan 's *my* partner. And there 's Uncle Salters and his manures, an' he reads Josephus. He 's sure I 'm crazy yet. And there 's poor little Penn, and he *is* crazy. You must n't talk to him about Johnstown, because—— And, oh, you *must* know Tom Platt and Long Jack and Manuel. Manuel saved my life. I 'm sorry he 's a Portugee. He can't talk much, but he 's an everlasting musician. He found me struck adrift and hauled me in."

"I wonder your nervous system is n't completely wrecked," said Mrs. Cheyne.

"What for, Mama? I worked like a horse and I ate like a hog and I slept like a dead man."

That was too much for Mrs. Cheyne, who began to think of her visions of a corpse rocking on the salty seas. She went to her state-room, and Harvey curled up beside his father, explaining his indebtedness.

"You can depend upon me to do everything I can for the crowd, Harve. They seem to be good men on your showing."

"Best in the Fleet, sir. Ask at Gloucester," said Harvey. "But Disko believes still he 's cured me of being crazy. Dan 's the only one I 've let on to about you, and our private cars and all the rest of it, and I 'm not *quite* sure Dan believes. I want to paralyze 'em to-morrow. Say, can't they run the 'Constance' over to Gloucester? Mama don't look fit to be moved, anyway, and we 're bound to finish cleaning out by to-morrow. Wouverman takes our fish. You see, we 're the first off the Banks this season, and it 's four twenty-five a quintal. We held out till he paid it. They want it quick."

"You mean you 'll have to work to-morrow, then?"

"I told Troop I would. I 'm on the scales. I 've brought the tallies with me." He looked at the greasy notebook with an air of importance that made his father choke. "There is n't but three—no—two ninety-four or five quintal more by my reckoning."

"Hire a substitute," suggested Cheyne, to see what Harvey would say.

"Can't, sir. I'm tally-man for the schooner. Troop says I've a better head for figures than Dan. Troop's a mighty just man."

"Well, suppose I don't move the 'Constance' to-night, how'll you fix it?"

Harvey looked at the clock, which marked twenty past eleven.

"Then I'll sleep here till three and catch the four o'clock freight. They let us men from the Fleet ride free as a rule."

"That's a notion. But I think we can get the 'Constance' around about as soon as your men's freight. Better go to bed now."

Harvey spread himself on the sofa, kicked off his boots, and was asleep before his father could shade the electrics. Cheyne sat watching the young face under the shadow of the arm thrown over the forehead, and among many things that occurred to him was the notion that he might perhaps have been neglectful as a father.

"One never knows when one's taking one's biggest risks," he said. "It might have been worse than drowning; but I don't think it has—I don't think it has. If it has n't, I have n't enough to pay Troop, that's all; and I don't think it has."

Morning brought a fresh sea breeze through the windows, the "Constance" was side-tracked among freight-cars at Gloucester, and Harvey had gone to his business.

"Then he'll fall overboard again and be drowned," the mother said bitterly.

"We'll go and look, ready to throw him a rope in case. You've never seen him working for his bread," said the father.

"What nonsense! As if any one expected——"

"Well, the man that hired him did. He's about right, too."

They went down between the stores full of fishermen's oilskins to Wouverman's wharf where the *We're Here* rode high, her Bank flag still flying, all hands busy as beavers in the glorious morning light. Disko stood by the main hatch superintending Manuel, Penn, and Uncle Salters at the tackle. Dan was swinging the loaded baskets inboard as Long Jack and Tom Platt filled them, and Harvey, with a notebook, represented the skipper's interests before the clerk of the scales on the salt-sprinkled wharf-edge.

"Ready!" cried the voices below. "Haul!" cried Disko. "Hi!" said Manuel. "Here!" said Dan, swinging the basket. Then they heard Harvey's voice, clear and fresh, checking the weights.

The last of the fish had been whipped out, and Harvey leaped from the string-piece six feet to a ratline, as the shortest way to hand Disko the tally, shouting, "Two ninety-seven, and an empty hold!"

"What 's the total, Harve?" said Disko.

"Eight sixty-five. Three thousand six hundred and seventy-six dollars *and* a quarter. 'Wish I 'd share as well as wage."

"Well, I won't go so far as to say you hev n't deserved it, Harve. Don't you want to slip up to Wouverman's office and take him our tallies?"

"Who 's that boy?" said Cheyne to Dan, well used to all manner of questions from those idle imbeciles called summer boarders.

"Well, he 's kind o' supercargo," was the answer. "We picked him up struck adrift on the Banks. Fell overboard from a liner, he sez. He was a passenger. He 's by way o' bein' a fisherman now."

"Is he worth his keep?"

"Ye-ep. Dad, this man wants to know ef Harve 's worth his keep. Say, would you like to go aboard? We 'll fix up a ladder for her."

"I should very much, indeed. 'T won't hurt you, Mama, and you 'll be able to see for yourself."

The woman who could not lift her head a week ago scrambled down the ladder, and stood aghast amid the mess and tangle aft.

"Be you anyways interested in Harve?" said Disko.

"Well, ye-es."

"He 's a good boy, an' ketches right hold jest as he 's bid. You 've heard haow we found him? He was sufferin' from nervous prostration, I guess, 'r else his head had hit somethin', when we hauled him aboard. He 's all over that naow. Yes, this is the cabin. 'T ain't anyways in order, but you 're quite welcome to look araound. Those are his figures on the stove-pipe, where we keep the reckonin' mostly."

"Did he sleep here?" said Mrs. Cheyne, sitting on a yellow locker and surveying the disorderly bunks.

"No. He berthed forward, madam, an' only fer him an' my boy hookin' fried pies an' muggin up when they ought to ha' been asleep, I dunno as I 've any special fault to find with him."

"There were n't nothin' wrong with Harve," said Uncle Salters, descending the steps. "He hung my boots on the main-truck, and he ain't over an' above respectful to such as knows more 'n he do, specially about farmin'; but he were mostly misled by Dan."

Dan in the meantime, profiting by dark hints from Harvey early that morning, was executing a war-dance on deck. "Tom, Tom!" he whispered down the hatch. "His folks has come, an' Dad hain't caught on yet, an' they 're pow-wowin' in the cabin. She 's a daisy, an' he 's all Harve claimed he was, by the looks of him."

"Howly Smoke!" said Long Jack, climbing out covered with salt and fish-skin. "D' ye belave his tale av the kid an' the little four-horse rig was thrue?"

"I knew it all along," said Dan. "Come an see Dad mistook in his judgments."

They came delightedly, just in time to hear Cheyne say: "I 'm glad he has a good character, because—he 's my son."

Disko's jaw fell,—Long Jack always vowed that he heard the click of it,—and he stared alternately at the man and the woman.

"I got his telegram in San Diego four days ago, and we came over."

"In a private car?" said Dan. "He said ye might."

"In a private car, of course."

Dan looked at his father with a hurricane of irreverent winks.

"There was a tale he told us av drivin' four little ponies in a rig av his own," said Long Jack. "Was that thrue now?"

"Very likely," said Cheyne. "Was it, Mama?"

"He had a little drag when we were in Toledo, I think," said the mother.

Long Jack whistled. "Oh, Disko!" said he, and that was all.

"I wuz—I am mistook in my jedgments—worse 'n the

men o' Marblehead," said Disko, as though the words were being windlassed out of him. "I don't mind ownin' to you, Mr. Cheyne, as I mistrusted the boy to be crazy. He talked kinder odd about money."

"So he told me."

"Did he tell ye anything else? 'Cause I pounded him once." This with a somewhat anxious glance at Mrs. Cheyne.

"Oh, yes," Cheyne replied. "I should say it probably did him more good than anything else in the world."

"I jedged 't wuz necessary, er I would n't ha' done it. I don't want you to think we abuse our boys any on this packet."

"I don't think you do, Mr. Troop."

Mrs. Cheyne had been looking at the faces—Disko's ivory-yellow, hairless, iron countenance; Uncle Salters's, with its rim of agricultural hair; Penn's bewildered simplicity; Manuel's quiet smile; Long Jack's grin of delight, and Tom Platt's scar. Rough, by her standards, they certainly were; but she had a mother's wits in her eyes, and she rose with out-stretched hands.

"Oh, tell me, which is who?" said she, half sobbing. "I want to thank you and bless you—all of you."

"Faith, that pays me a hunder time," said Long Jack.

Disko introduced them all in due form. The captain of an old-time Chinaman could have done no better, and Mrs. Cheyne babbled incoherently. She nearly threw herself into Manuel's arms when she understood that he had first found Harvey.

"But how *shall* I leave him dreeft?" said poor Manuel. "What do you yourself if you find him so? Eh, wha-at? We are in one good boy, and I am *ever* so pleased he come to be your son."

"And he told me Dan was his partner!" she cried. Dan was already sufficiently pink, but he turned a rich crimson when Mrs. Cheyne kissed him on both cheeks before the assembly. Then they led her forward to show her the foc'sle, at which she wept again, and must needs go down to see Harvey's identical bunk, and there she found the Negro cook cleaning up the stove, and he nodded as though she were someone he had expected to meet for years. They tried, two at a time, to explain the boat's daily life to her, and she sat by the pawl-post, her gloved hands on the greasy table, laughing with trembling lips and crying with dancing eyes.

"And who 's ever to use the *We 're Here* after this?" said Long Jack to Tom Platt. "I feel as if she 'd made a cathedral av ut all."

"Cathedral!" sneered Tom Platt. "Oh, ef it had bin even the Fish C'mmission boat instid of this bally-hoo o' blazes. Ef we only hed some decency an' order an' side-boys when she goes over! She 'll have to climb that ladder like a hen, an' we—we ought to be mannin' the yards!"

"Then Harvey was *not* mad," said Penn, slowly, to Cheyne.

"No, indeed—thank God," the big millionaire replied, stooping down tenderly.

"It must be terrible to be mad. Except to lose your child, I do not know anything more terrible. But your child has come back? Let us thank God for that."

"Hello!" cried Harvey, looking down upon them benignly from the wharf.

"I wuz mistook, Harve. I wuz mistook," said Disko, swiftly, holding up a hand. "I wuz mistook in my jedgments. Ye need n't rub in any more."

"Guess I'll take care o' that," said Dan, under his breath.

"You 'll be goin' off naow, won't ye?"

"Well, not without the balance of my wages, 'less you want to have the *We 're Here* attached."

"Thet 's so; I 'd clean forgot"; and he counted out the remaining dollars. "You done all you contracted to do, Harve; and you done it 'baout 's well as ef you 'd been brought up——" Here Disko brought himself up. He did not quite see where the sentence was going to end.

"Outside of a private car?" suggested Dan, wickedly.

"Come on, and I'll show her to you," said Harvey.

Cheyne stayed to talk with Disko, but the others made a procession to the depot, with Mrs. Cheyne at the head. The French maid shrieked at the invasion; and Harvey laid the glories of the "Constance" before them without a word. They took them in equal silence—stamped leather, silver door-handles and rails, cut velvet, plate-glass, nickel, bronze, hammered iron, and the rare woods of the continent inlaid.

"I told you," said Harvey; "I told you." This was his crowning revenge, and a most ample one.

Mrs. Cheyne decreed a meal, and that nothing might be lacking to the tale Long Jack told afterwards in his boarding-house, she waited on them herself. Men who are accustomed to eat at tiny tables in howling gales have curiously neat and finished manners; but Mrs. Cheyne, who did not know this, was surprised. She longed to have Manuel for a butler; so silently and easily did he comport himself among the frail glassware and dainty silver. Tom Platt remembered the great days on the *Ohio* and the manners of foreign potentates who dined with the officers; and Long Jack, being Irish, supplied the small talk till all were at their ease.

In the *We 're Here's* cabin the fathers took stock of each other behind their cigars. Cheyne knew well enough when he dealt with a man to whom he could not offer money; equally well he knew that no money could pay for what Disko had done. He kept his own counsel and waited for an opening.

"I hev n't done anything *to* your boy or *fer* your boy excep' make him work a piece an' learn him how to handle the hog-yoke," said Disko. "He has twice my boy's head for figgers."

"By the way," Cheyne answered casually, "what d' you calculate to make of your boy?"

Disko removed his cigar and waved it comprehensively round the cabin. "Dan 's jest plain boy, an' he don't allow me to do any of his thinkin'. He 'll hev this able little packet when I 'm laid by. He ain't noways anxious to quit the business. I know that."

"Mmm! 'Ever been West, Mr. Troop?"

" 'Bin 's fer ez Noo York once in a boat. I 've no use for railroads. No more hez Dan. Salt water 's good enough fer the Troops. I 've ben 'most everywhere—in the nat'ral way, o' course."

"I can give him all the salt water he 's likely to need—till he 's a skipper."

"Haow 's that? I thought you wuz a kinder railroad king. Harve told me so when—I was mistook in my jedgments."

"We 're all apt to be mistaken. I fancied perhaps you might know I own a line of tea-clippers—San Francisco to Yokohama—six of 'em—iron-built, about seventeen hundred and eighty tons apiece."

"Blame that boy! He never told. I 'd ha' listened to *that,* instid o' his truck abaout railroads an' pony-carriages."

"He did n't know."

" 'Little thing like that slipped his mind, I guess."

"No, I only capt—took hold of the 'Blue M.' freighters —Morgan and McQuade's old line—this summer."

Disko collapsed where he sat, beside the stove.

"Great Cæsar Almighty! I mistrust I 've ben fooled from one end to the other. Why, Phil Airheart he went from this very town six year back—no, seven—an' he 's mate on the *San José* now—twenty-six days was her time out. His sister she 's livin' here yet, an' she reads his letters to my woman. An' *you* own the 'Blue M.' freighters?"

Cheyne nodded.

"If I 'd known that I 'd ha' jerked the *We 're Here* back to port all standin', on the word."

"Perhaps that would n't have been so good for Harvey."

"Ef I 'd only known! Ef he 'd only *said* about the cussed Line, I 'd ha' understood! I 'll never stand on my own jedgments again—never. They 're well-found packets. Phil Airheart he says so."

"I 'm glad to have a recommend from that quarter. Airheart 's skipper of the *San José* now. What I was getting at is to know whether you 'd lend me Dan for a year or two, and we 'll see if we can't make a mate of him. Would you trust him to Airheart?"

"It 's a resk taking a raw boy——"

"I know a man who did more for me."

"That 's diff'runt. Look at here naow, I ain't recommendin' Dan special because he 's my own flesh an' blood. *I* know Bank ways ain't clipper ways, but he hain't much to learn. Steer he can—no boy better, ef *I* say it—an' the rest 's in our blood an' get; but I could wish he war n't so cussed weak on navigation."

"Airheart will attend to that. He 'll ship as boy for a voyage or two, and then we can put him in the way of doing better. Suppose you take him in hand this winter, and I'll send for him early in the spring. I know the Pacific 's a long ways off——"

"Pshaw! We Troops, livin' an' dead, are all around the earth an' the seas thereof."

"But I want you to understand—and I mean this—any time you think you 'd like to see him, tell me, and I 'll attend to the transportation. 'T won't cost you a cent."

"Ef you 'll walk a piece with me, we 'll go to my house an' talk this to my woman. I 've bin so crazy mistook in all my jedgments, it don't seem to me this was like to be real."

They went over to Troop's eighteen-hundred-dollar, blue-trimmed white house, with a retired dory full of nasturtiums in the front yard and a shuttered parlour which was a museum of overseas plunder. There sat a large woman, silent and grave, with the dim eyes of those who look long to the sea for the return of their beloved. Cheyne addressed himself to her, and she gave consent wearily.

"We lose one hundred a year from Gloucester only, Mr. Cheyne," she said—"one hundred boys an' men; an' I 've come so 's to hate the sea as if't wuz alive an' listenin'. God never made it fer humans to anchor on. These packets o' yours they go straight out, I take it, and straight home again?"

"As straight as the winds let 'em, and I give a bonus for record passages. Tea don't improve by being at sea."

"When he wuz little he used to play at keeping store, an' I had hopes he might follow that up. But soon 's he could paddle a dory I knew that were goin' to be denied me."

"They 're square-riggers, Mother; iron-built an' well found. Remember what Phil's sister reads you when she gits his letters."

"I 've never known as Phil told lies, but he 's too venturesome (like most of 'em that use the sea). Ef Dan sees fit, Mr. Cheyne, he can go—fer all o' me."

"She jest despises the ocean," Disko explained, "an' I —I dunno haow to act polite, I guess, er I 'd thank you better."

"My father—my own eldest brother—two nephews— an' my second sister's man," she said, dropping her head on her hands. "Would *you* care fer any one that took all those?"

Cheyne was relieved when Dan turned up and accepted with more delight than he was able to put into words. Indeed, the offer meant a plain and sure road to all desirable things; but Dan thought most of commanding watch on broad decks, and looking into far-away harbours.

Mrs. Cheyne had spoken privately to the unaccountable Manuel in the matter of Harvey's rescue. He seemed to have no desire for money. Pressed hard, he said that he would take five dollars, because he wanted to buy something for a girl. Otherwise—"How shall I take money when I make so easy my eats and smokes? You *will* giva some if I like or no? Eh, wha-at? Then you shall giva me money, but not that way. You shall giva all you can think." He introduced her to a snuffy Portuguese priest with a list of semi-destitute widows as long as his cassock. As a strict Unitarian, Mrs. Cheyne could not sympathize with the creed, but she ended by respecting the brown, voluble little man.

Manuel, faithful son of the Church, appropriated all the blessings showered on her for her charity. "That letta me out," said he. "I have now ver' good absolutions for six months"; and he strolled forth to get a handkerchief for the girl of the hour and to break the hearts of all the others.

Salters went West for a season with Penn, and left no address behind. He had a dread that these millionry people, with wasteful private cars, might take undue interest in his companion. It was better to visit inland relatives till the coast was clear. "Never you be adopted by rich folk, Penn," he said in the cars, "or I 'll take 'n' break this checker-board over your head. Ef you forget your name again—which is Pratt—you remember you belong with Salters Troop, an' set down right where you are till I come fer you. Don't go taggin' araound after them whose eyes bung out with fatness, accordin' to Scripcher."

# CHAPTER X

BUT IT WAS otherwise with the *We 're Here's* silent cook, for he came up, his kit in his handkerchief, and boarded the "Constance." Pay was no particular object, and he did not in the least care where he slept. His business, as revealed to him in dreams, was to follow Harvey for the rest of his days. They tried argument and, at last, persuasion; but there is a difference between one Cape Breton and two Alabama Negroes, and the matter was referred to Cheyne by the cook and porter. The millionaire only laughed. He presumed Harvey might need a body-servant some day or other, and was sure that one volunteer was worth five hirelings. Let the man stay, therefore; even though he called himself MacDonald and swore in Gaelic. The car could go back to Boston, where, if he were still of the same mind, they would take him West.

With the "Constance," which in his heart of hearts he loathed, departed the last remnant of Cheyne's millionairedom, and he gave himself up to an energetic idleness. This Gloucester was a new town in a new land, and he proposed to "take it in," as of old he had taken in all the cities from Snohomish to San Diego of that world whence he hailed. They made money along the crooked street which was half wharf and half ship's store: as a leading professional he wished to learn how the noble game was played. Men said that four out of every five fish-balls served at New England's Sunday breakfast came from Gloucester, and overwhelmed him with figures in proof—statistics of boats, gear, wharf-frontage, capital invested, salting, packing, factories, insurance, wages, repairs, and profits. He talked with the owners of the large fleets whose skippers were little more than hired men, and whose crews were almost all Swedes or Portuguese. Then he conferred with Disko, one of the few who owned their craft, and compared notes in his vast head. He coiled himself away on chain-cables in marine junk-shops, asking

questions with cheerful, unslaked Western curiosity, till
all the water-front wanted to know "what in thunder that
man was after, anyhow." He prowled into the Mutual
Insurance rooms, and demanded explanations of the mysterious remarks chalked up on the blackboard day by day;
and that brought down upon him secretaries of every
Fisherman's Widow and Orphan Aid Society within the
city limits. They begged shamelessly, each man anxious
to beat the other institution's record, and Cheyne tugged
at his beard and handed them all over to Mrs. Cheyne.

She was resting in a boarding-house near Eastern Point—a
strange establishment, managed, apparently, by the boarders,
where the table-cloths were red-and-white-checkered and
the population, who seemed to have known one another
intimately for years, rose up at midnight to make Welsh
rarebits if it felt hungry. On the second morning of her
stay Mrs. Cheyne put away her diamond solitaires before
she came down to breakfast.

"They 're most delightful people," she confided to her
husband; "so friendly and simple, too, though they are all
Boston, nearly."

"That is n't simpleness, Mama," he said, looking across
the boulders behind the apple-trees where the hammocks
were slung. "It 's the other thing, that we—that I have n't
got."

"It can't be," said Mrs. Cheyne quietly. "There is n't
a woman here owns a dress that cost a hundred dollars.
Why, we——"

"I know it, dear. We have—of course we have. I guess
it 's only the style they wear East. Are you having a good
time?"

"I don't see very much of Harvey; he 's always with you;
but I ain't near as nervous as I was."

"I have n't had such a good time since Willie died. I
never rightly understood that I had a son before this.
Harve 's got to be a great boy. Anything I can fetch you,
dear? Cushion under your head? Well, we 'll go down to
the wharf again and look around."

Harvey was his father's shadow in those days, and the
two strolled along side by side, Cheyne using the grades
as an excuse for laying his hand on the boy's square shoul-

der. It was then that Harvey noticed and admired what had never struck him before—his father's curious power of getting at the heart of new matters as learned from men in the street.

"How d' you make 'em tell you everything without opening your head?" demanded the son, as they came out of a rigger's loft.

"I 've dealt with quite a few men in my time, Harve, and one sizes 'em up somehow, I guess. I know something about myself, too." Then, after a pause, as they sat down on a wharf-edge: "Men can 'most always tell when a man has handled things for himself, and then they treat him as one of themselves."

"Same as they treat me down at Wouverman's wharf. I 'm one of the crowd now. Disko has told every one I 've earned my pay." Harvey spread out his hands and rubbed the palms together. "They 're all soft again," he said dolefully.

"Keep 'em that way for the next few years, while you 're getting your education. You can harden 'em up after."

"Ye-es, I suppose so," was the reply, in no delighted voice.

"It rests with you, Harve. You can take cover behind your mama, of course, and put her on to fussing about your nerves and your high-strungness and all that kind of poppy-cock."

"Have I ever done that?" said Harvey, uneasily.

His father turned where he sat and thrust out a long hand. "*You* know as well as I do that I can't make anything of you if you don't act straight by me. I can handle you alone if you 'll stay alone, but I don't pretend to manage both you *and* Mama. Life's too short, anyway."

"Don't make me out much of a fellow, does it?"

"I guess it was my fault a good deal; but if you want the truth, you have n't been much of anything up to date. Now, have you?"

"Umm! Disko thinks . . . Say, what d' you reckon it 's cost you to raise me from the start—first, last and all over?"

Cheyne smiled. "I 've never kept track, but I should estimate, in dollars and cents, nearer fifty than forty thousand; maybe sixty. The young generation comes high. It has to have things, and it tires of 'em, and—the old man foots the bill."

Harvey whistled, but at heart he was rather pleased to think that his upbringing had cost so much. "And all that 's sunk capital, is n't it?"

"Invested, Harve. Invested, I hope."

"Making it only thirty thousand, the thirty I've earned is about ten cents on the hundred. That 's a mighty poor catch." Harvey wagged his head solemnly.

Cheyne laughed till he nearly fell off the pile into the water.

"Disko has got a heap more than that out of Dan since he was ten; and Dan' s at school half the year, too."

"Oh, that 's what you 're after, is it?"

"No. I 'm not after anything. I 'm not stuck on myself any just now—that 's all. . . . I ought to be kicked."

"I can't do it, old man; or I would, I presume, if I 'd been made that way."

"Then I 'd have remembered it to the last day I lived— and *never* forgiven you," said Harvey, his chin on his doubled fists.

"Exactly. That 's about what I 'd do. You see?"

"I see. The fault's with me and no one else. All the samey, something 's got to be done about it."

Cheyne drew a cigar from his vest-pocket, bit off the end, and fell to smoking. Father and son were very much alike; for the beard hid Cheyne's mouth, and Harvey had his father's slightly aquiline nose, close-set black eyes, and narrow, high cheek-bones. With a touch of brown paint he would have made up very picturesquely as a Red Indian of the story-books.

"Now you can go on from here," said Cheyne, slowly, "costing me between six or eight thousand a year till you 're a voter. Well, we 'll call you a man then. You can go right on from *that*, living on me to the tune of forty or fifty thousand, besides what your mother will give you, with a valet and a yacht or a fancy-ranch where you can pretend to raise trotting-stock and play cards with your own crowd."

"Like Lorry Tuck?" Harvey put in.

"Yep; or the two De Vitré boys or old man McQuade 's

"His father turned where he sat and thrust out a long hand.
'*You* know as well as I do that I can't make anything of
you if you don't act straight by me.'"

son. California 's full of 'em, and here 's an Eastern sample while we 're talking."

A shiny black steam-yacht, with mahogany deck-house, nickel-plated binnacles, and pink-and-white-striped awnings puffed up the harbour, flying the burgee of some New York club. Two young men in what they conceived to be sea costumes were playing cards by the saloon skylight; and a couple of women with red and blue parasols looked on and laughed noisily.

"Should n't care to be caught out in her in any sort of a breeze. No beam," said Harvey, critically, as the yacht slowed to pick up her mooring-buoy.

"They 're having what stands them for a good time. I can give you that, and twice as much as that, Harve. How 'd you like it?"

"Cæsar! That 's no way to get a dinghy overside," said Harvey, still intent on the yacht. "If I could n't slip a tackle better than that I 'd stay ashore. . . . What if I don't?"

"Stay ashore—or what?"

"Yacht and ranch and live on 'the old man,' and—get behind Mama when there 's trouble," said Harvey, with a twinkle in his eye.

"Why, in that case, you come right in with me, my son."

"Ten dollars a month?" Another twinkle.

"Not a cent more until you 're worth it, and you won't begin to touch that for a few years."

"I 'd sooner begin sweeping out the office—is n't that how the big bugs start?—and touch something now than——"

"I know it; we all feel that way. But I guess we can hire any sweeping we need. I made the same mistake myself of starting in too soon."

"Thirty million dollars' worth o' mistake, was n't it? I 'd risk it for that."

"I lost some; and I gained some. I'll tell you."

Cheyne pulled his beard and smiled as he looked over the still water, and spoke away from Harvey, who presently began to be aware that his father was telling the story of his life. He talked in a low, even voice, without gesture and without expression; and it was a history for which a dozen leading journalists would cheerfully have paid many dollars—the story of forty years that was at the same time the story of the New West, whose story is yet to be written.

It began with a kinless boy turned loose in Texas, and went on fantastically through a hundred changes and chops of life, the scenes shifting from State after Western State, from cities that sprang up in a month and in a season utterly withered away, to wild ventures in wilder camps that are now laborious, paved municipalities. It covered the building of three railroads and the deliberate wreck of a fourth. It told of steamers, townships, forests, and mines, and the men of every nation under heaven, manning, creating, hewing, and digging these. It touched on chances of gigantic wealth flung before eyes that could not see, or missed by the merest accident of time and travel; and through the mad shift of things, sometimes on horseback, more often afoot, now rich, now poor, in and out, and back and forth, deck-hand, train-hand, contractor, boarding-house keeper, journalist, engineer, drummer, real-estate agent, politician, dead-beat, rum-seller, mine-owner, speculator, cattle-man, or tramp, moved Harvey Cheyne, alert and quiet, seeking his own ends, and, so he said, the glory and advancement of his country.

He told of the faith that never deserted him even when he hung on the ragged edge of despair—the faith that comes of knowing men and things. He enlarged, as though he were talking to himself, on his very great courage and resource at all times. The thing was so evident in the man's mind that he never even changed his tone. He described how he had bested his enemies, or forgiven them, exactly as they had bested or forgiven him in those careless days; how he had entreated, cajoled, and bullied towns, companies, and syndicates, all for their enduring good; crawled round, through, or under mountains and ravines, dragging a string and hoop-iron railroad after him, and in the end, how he had sat still while promiscuous communities tore the last fragments of his character to shreds.

The tale held Harvey almost breathless, his head a little cocked to one side, his eyes fixed on his father's face, as the twilight deepened and the red cigar-end lit up the furrowed cheeks and heavy eyebrows. It seemed to him like watching a locomotive storming across country in the dark—a mile between each glare of the open fire-door: but this locomotive could talk, and the words shook and stirred the boy to the core of his soul. At last Cheyne pitched away the cigar-butt, and the two sat in the dark over the lapping water.

"I 've never told that to anyone before," said the father.

Harvey gasped. "It 's just the greatest thing that ever was!" said he.

"That 's what I *got*. Now I 'm coming to what I did n't get. It won't sound much of anything to you, but I don't wish you to be as old as I am before you find out. I can handle men, of course, and I 'm no fool along my own lines, but—but—I can't compete with the man who has been *taught*! I 've picked up as I went along, and I guess it sticks out all over me."

"I 've never seen it," said the son, indignantly.

"You will, though, Harve. You will—just as soon as you 're through college. Don't I know it? Don't I know the look on men's faces when they think me a—a 'mucker,' as they call it out here? I can break them to little pieces —yes—but I can't get back at 'em to hurt 'em where they live. I don't say they 're 'way 'way up, but I feel I 'm 'way, 'way, 'way off, somehow. Now *you 've* got your chance. You 've got to soak up all the learning that 's around, and you 'll live with a crowd that are doing the same thing. They 'll be doing it for a few thousand dollars a year at most; but remember *you 'll* be doing it for millions. You 'll learn law enough to look after your own property when I 'm out o' light, and you 'll have to be solid with the best men in the market (they are useful later); and above all, you 'll have to stow away the plain, common, sit-down-with-your-chin-on-your-elbows book-learning. Nothing pays like that, Harve, and it 's bound to pay more and more each year in our country—in business *and* in politics. You 'll see."

"There 's no sugar my end of the deal," said Harvey. "Four years at college! 'Wish I 'd chosen the valet and the yacht!"

"Never mind, my son," Cheyne insisted. "You 're in-vesting your capital where it 'll bring in the best returns; and I guess you won't find our property shrunk any when you 're ready to take hold. Think it over, and let me know in the morning. Hurry! We 'll be late for supper!"

As this was a business talk, there was no need for Harvey to tell his mother about it; and Cheyne naturally took the same point of view. But Mrs. Cheyne saw and feared, and was a little jealous. Her boy, who rode rough-shod over her, was gone, and in his stead reigned a keen-faced youth, abnormally silent, who addressed most of his conversation to his father. She understood it was business, and therefore a matter beyond her premises. If she had any doubts, they were resolved when Cheyne went to Boston and brought back a new diamond marquise ring.

· "What have you two been doing now?" she said, with a weak little smile, as she turned it in the light.

"Talking—just talking, Mama; there 's nothing mean about Harvey."

There was not. The boy had made a treaty on his own account. Railroads, he explained gravely, interested him as little as lumber, real estate, or mining. What his soul yearned after was control of his father's newly purchased sailing-ships. If that could be promised him within what he conceived to be a reasonable time, he, for his part, guaranteed diligence and sobriety at college for four or five years. In vacation he was to be allowed full access to all details connected with the line—he had not asked more than two thousand questions about it—from his father's most private papers in the safe to the tug in San Francisco harbour.

"It 's a deal," said Cheyne at the last. "You 'll alter your mind twenty times before you leave college, o' course; but if you take hold of it in proper shape, and if you don't tie it up before you 're twenty-three, I 'll make the thing over to you. How 's that, Harve?"

"Nope; never pays to split up a going concern. There 's too much competition in the world anyway, and Disko says 'blood-kin *hev* to stick together.' His crowd never go back on him. That 's one reason, he says, why they make such big fares. Say, the *We 're Here* goes off to the Georges on Monday. They don't stay long ashore, do they?"

"Well, we ought to be going, too, I guess. I 've left my business hung up at loose ends between two oceans, and it 's time to connect again. I just hate to do it, though; have n't had a holiday like this for twenty years."

"We *can't* go without seeing Disko off," said Harvey; "and Monday 's Memorial Day. Let 's stay over that, anyway."

"What is this memorial business? They were talking about it at the boarding-house," said Cheyne weakly. He, too, was not anxious to spoil the golden days.

"Well, as far as I can make out, *this* business is a sort of song-and-dance act, whacked up for the summer boarders. Disko don't think much of it, he says, because they take up a collection for the widows and orphans. Disko's independent. Have n't you noticed that?"

"Well—yes. A little. In spots. Is it a town show, then?"

"The summer convention is. They read out the names of the fellows drowned or gone astray since last time, and they make speeches, and recite, and all. Then, Disko says, the secretaries of the Aid Societies go into the back yard and fight over the catch. The real show, he says, is in the spring. The ministers all take a hand then, and there are n't any summer boarders around."

"I see," said Cheyne, with the brilliant and perfect comprehension of one born into and bred up to city pride. "We 'll stay over for Memorial Day, and get off in the afternoon."

"Guess I 'll go down to Disko's and make him bring his crowd up before they sail. I 'll have to stand with them, of course."

"Oh, that 's it, is it," said Cheyne. "I 'm only a poor summer boarder, and you 're——"

"A Banker—full-blooded Banker," Harvey called back as he boarded a trolley, and Cheyne went on with his blissful dreams for the future.

Disko had no use for public functions where appeals were made for charity, but Harvey pleaded that the glory of the day would be lost, so far as he was concerned, if the *We 're Heres* absented themselves. Then Disko made conditions. He had heard—it was astonishing how all the world knew all the world's business along the water-front —he had heard that a "Philadelphia actress-woman" was going to take part in the exercises; and he mistrusted that she would deliver "Skipper Ireson's Ride." Personally, he had as little use for actresses as for summer boarders; but justice was justice, and though he himself (here Dan giggled) had once slipped up on a matter of judgment, this thing must not be. So Harvey came back to East Gloucester, and spent half a day explaining to an amused actress with a royal reputation on two seaboards the inwardness of the mistake she contemplated; and she admitted that it was justice, even as Disko had said.

Cheyne knew by old experience what would happen; but anything of the nature of a public palaver was meat and drink to the man's soul. He saw the trolleys hurrying west, in the hot, hazy morning, full of women in light summer dresses and white-faced straw-hatted men fresh from Boston desks; the stack of bicycles outside the post-office; the come-and-go of busy officials, greeting one another; the slow flick and swash of bunting in the heavy air; and the important man with a hose sluicing the brick sidewalk.

"Mother," he said suddenly, "don't you remember— after Seattle was burned out—and they got her going again?"

Mrs. Cheyne nodded, and looked critically down the crooked street. Like her husband, she understood these gatherings, all the West over, and compared them one against another. The fishermen began to mingle with the crowd about the town-hall doors—blue-jowled Portuguese, their women bare-headed or shawled for the most part; clear-eyed Nova Scotians, and men of the Maritime Provinces; French, Italians, Swedes, and Danes, with outside crews of coasting schooners; and everywhere women in black, who saluted one another with gloomy pride, for this was their day of great days. And there were ministers of many creeds,—pastors of great, gilt-edged congregations, at the seaside for a rest, with shepherds of the regular work,—from the priests of the Church on the Hill to bush-bearded ex-sailor Lutherans, hail-fellow with the men of a score of boats. There were owners of lines of schooners, large contributors to the societies, and small men, their few craft pawned to the mastheads, with bankers and marine-insurance agents, captains of tugs and water-boats, riggers, fitters, lumpers, salters, boat-builders, and coopers, and all the mixed population of the water-front.

They drifted along the line of seats made gay with the dresses of the summer boarders, and one of the town officials patrolled and perspired till he shone all over with pure civic pride. Cheyne had met him for five minutes a few days before, and between the two there was entire understanding.

"Well, Mr. Cheyne, and what 'd you think of our city? —Yes, madam, you can sit anywhere you please.—You have this kind of thing out West, I presume?"

"Yes, but we are n't as old as you."

"That 's so, of course. You ought to have been at the exercises when we celebrated our two hundred and fiftieth birthday. I tell you, Mr. Cheyne, the old city did herself credit."

"So I heard. It pays, too. What 's the matter with the town that it don't have a first-class hotel, though?"

"—Right over there to the left, Pedro. Heaps o' room for you and your crowd.—Why, that 's what I tell 'em all the time, Mr. Cheyne. There 's big money in it, but I presume that don't affect you any. What we want is——"

A heavy hand fell on his broadcloth shoulder, and the flushed skipper of a Portland coal-and-ice coaster spun him half round. "What in thunder do you fellows mean by clappin' the law on the town when all decent men are at sea this way? Heh? Town's dry as a bone, an' smells a sight worse sence I quit. 'Might ha' left us one saloon for soft drinks, anyway."

"Don't seem to have hindered your nourishment this morning, Carsen. I 'll go into the politics of it later. Sit down by the door and think over your arguments till I come back."

"What good is arguments to me? In Miquelon champagne's eighteen dollars a case and——" The skipper lurched into his seat as an organ-prelude silenced him.

"Our new organ," said the official proudly to Cheyne. "'Cost us four thousand dollars, too. We 'll have to get back to high-license next year to pay for it. I was n't going to let the ministers have all the religion at their convention. Those are some of our orphans standing up to sing. My wife taught 'em. See you again later, Mr. Cheyne. I 'm wanted on the platform."

High, clear, and true, children's voices bore down the last noise of those settling into their places.

*"O all ye Works of the Lord, bless ye the Lord: praise him and magnify him for ever!"*

The women throughout the hall leaned forward to look as the reiterated cadences filled the air. Mrs. Cheyne, with some others, began to breathe short; she had hardly imagined there were so many widows in the world; and instinctively searched for Harvey. He had found the *We 're Heres* at the back of the audience, and was standing, as by right, between Dan and Disko. Uncle Salters, returned the night before with Penn, from Pamlico Sound, received him suspiciously.

"Hain't your folk gone yet?" he grunted. "What are you doin' here, young feller?"

*"O ye Seas and Floods, bless ye the Lord: praise him, and magnify him for ever!"*

"Hain't he good right?" said Dan. "He 's bin there, same as the rest of us."

"Not in them clothes," Salters snarled.

"Shut your head, Salters," said Disko. "Your bile 's gone back on you. Stay right where ye are, Harve."

Then up and spoke the orator of the occasion, another pillar of the municipality, bidding the world welcome to Gloucester, and incidentally pointing out wherein Gloucester excelled the rest of the world. Then he turned to the sea-wealth of the city, and spoke of the price that must be paid for the yearly harvest. They would hear later the names of their lost dead—one hundred and seventeen of them. (The widows stared a little, and looked at one another here.) Gloucester could not boast any overwhelming mills or factories. Her sons worked for such wage as the sea gave; and they all knew that neither Georges nor the Banks were cow-pastures. The utmost that folk ashore could accomplish was to help the widows and the orphans, and after a few general remarks he took this opportunity of thanking, in the name of the city, those who had so public-spiritedly consented to participate in the exercises of the occasion.

"I jest despise the beggin' pieces in it," growled Disko. "It don't give folk a fair notion of us."

"Ef folk won't be fore-handed an' put by when they 've the chance," returned Salters, "it stands in the nature o' things they *hev* to be 'shamed. You take warnin' by that, young feller. Riches endureth but for a season, ef you scatter them araound on lugsuries——"

"But to lose everything, everything," said Penn. "What can you do *then?* Once I"—the watery blue eyes stared up and down as if looking for something to steady them —"once I read—in a book, I think—of a boat where every one was run down—except some one—and he said to me——"

"Shucks!" said Salters, cutting in. "You read a little less an' take more int'rust in your vittles, and you 'll come nearer earnin' your keep, Penn."

Harvey, jammed among the fishermen, felt a creepy, crawly, tingling thrill that began in the back of his neck and ended at his boots. He was cold, too, though it was a stifling day.

"'That the actress from Philadelphia?" said Disko Troop, scowling at the platform. "You 've fixed it about old man Ireson, hain't ye, Harve? Ye know why naow."

It was not "Ireson's Ride" that the woman delivered, but some sort of poem about a fishing-port called Brixham and a fleet of trawlers beating in against storm by night, while the women made a guiding fire at the head of the quay with everything they could lay hands on.

> "They took the grandma's blanket,
>   Who shivered and bade them go;
> They took the baby's cradle,
>   Who could not say them no."

"Whew!" said Dan, peering over Long Jack's shoulder. "That's great! Must ha' bin expensive, though."

"Ground-hog case," said the Galway man. "Badly lighted port, Danny."

> "And knew not all the while
> If they were lighting a bonfire
> Or only a funeral pile."

The wonderful voice took hold of people by their heart-strings; and when she told how the drenched crews were flung ashore, living and dead, and they carried the bodies to the glare of the fires, asking: "Child, is this your father?" or "Wife, is this your man?" you could hear hard breathing all over the benches.

> "And when the boats of Brixham
>    Go out to face the gales,
> Think of the love that travels
>    Like light upon their sails!"

There was very little applause when she finished. The women were looking for their handkerchiefs, and many of the men stared at the ceiling with shiny eyes.

"H'm," said Salters; "that 'u'd cost ye a dollar to hear at any theatre—maybe two. Some folk, I presoom, can afford it. 'Seems downright waste to me. . . . Naow, how in Jerusalem did Cap Bart Edwardes strike adrift here?"

"No keepin' him under," said an Eastport man behind. "He's a poet, an' he 's baound to say his piece. 'Comes from daown aour way, too."

He did not say that Captain B. Edwardes had striven for five consecutive years to be allowed to recite a piece of his own composition on Gloucester Memorial Day. An amused and exhausted committee had at last given him his desire. The simplicity and utter happiness of the old man, as he stood up in his very best Sunday clothes, won the audience ere he opened his mouth. They sat unmurmuring through seven-and-thirty hatchet-made verses describing at fullest length the loss of the schooner *Joan Hasken* off the Georges in the gale of 1867, and when he came to an end they shouted with one kindly throat.

A far-sighted Boston reporter slid away for a full copy of the epic and an interview with the author; so that earth had nothing more to offer Captain Bart Edwardes, ex-whaler, shipwright, master-fisherman, and poet, in the seventy-third year of his age.

"Naow, I call that sensible," said the Eastport man. "I 've bin over that graound with his writin', jest as he read it, in my two hands, and I can testify that he 's got it all in."

"If Dan here could n't do better 'n that with one hand before breakfast, he ought to be switched," said Salters, upholding the honour of Massachusetts on general principles. "Not but what I 'm free to own he 's considerable litt'ery—fer Maine. Still——"

"Guess Uncle Salters's goin' to die this trip. Fust compliment he 's ever paid me," Dan sniggered. "What 's wrong with you, Harve? You act all quiet and you look greenish. Feelin' sick?"

"Don't know what 's the matter with me," Harvey replied." " 'Seems if my insides were too big for my outsides. I 'm all crowded up and shivery."

"Dispepsy? Pshaw—too bad. We 'll wait for the readin', an' then we 'll quit, an' catch the tide."

The widows—they were nearly all of that season's making—braced themselves rigidly like people going to be shot in cold blood, for they knew what was coming. The summer-boarder girls in pink and blue shirt-waists stopped tittering over Captain Edwardes's wonderful poem, and looked back to see why all was silent. The fishermen pressed forward as that town official who had talked to Cheyne bobbed up on the platform and began to read the year's list of losses, dividing them into months. Last September's casualties were mostly single men and strangers, but his voice rang very loud in the stillness of the hall.

"September 9th.—Schooner *Florrie Anderson* lost, with all aboard, off the Georges.
"Reuben Pitman, master, 50, single, Main Street, City.
"Emil Olsen, 19, single, 329 Hammond Street, City. Denmark.
"Oscar Standberg, single, 25. Sweden.
"Carl Stanberg, single, 28, Main Street. City.
"Pedro, supposed Madeira, single, Keene's boarding-house. City.
"Joseph Welsh, alias Joseph Wright, 30, St. John's, Newfoundland."

"No—Augusty, Maine," a voice cried from the body of the hall.

"He shipped from St. John's," said the reader, looking to see.

"I know it. He belongs in Augusty. My nevvy."

The reader made a pencilled correction on the margin of the list, and resumed

"Same schooner, Charlie Richie, Liverpool, Nova Scotia, 33, single.

"Albert May, 267 Rogers Street, City, 27, single.

"September 27th.—Orvin Dollard, 30, married, drowned in dory off Eastern Point."

That shot went home, for one of the widows flinched where she sat, clasping and unclasping her hands. Mrs. Cheyne, who had been listening with wide-opened eyes, threw up her head and choked. Dan's mother, a few seats to the right, saw and heard and quickly moved to her side. The reading went on. By the time they reached the January and February wrecks the shots were falling thick and fast, and the widows drew breath between their teeth.

"February 14th.—Schooner *Harry Randolph* dismasted on the way home form Newfoundland; Asa Musie, married, 32, Main Street, City, lost overboard.

"February 23d.—Schooner *Gilbert Hope;* went astray in dory, Robert Beavon, 29, married, native of Pubnico, Nova Scotia."

But his wife was in the hall. They heard a low cry, as though a little animal had been hit. It was stifled at once, and a girl staggered out of the hall. She had been hoping against hope for months, because some who have gone adrift in dories have been miraculously picked up by deep-sea sailing-ships. Now she had her certainty, and Harvey could see the policeman on the sidewalk hailing a hack for her. "It's fifty cents to the depot"—the driver began, but the policeman held up his hand—"but I 'm goin' there anyway. Jump right in. Look at here, Alf; you don't pull me next time my lamps ain't lit. See?"

The side-door closed on the patch of bright sunshine, and Harvey's eyes turned again to the reader and his endless list.

"April 19th.—Schooner *Mamie Douglas* lost on the Banks with all hands.

"Edward Canton, 43, master, married, City.

"D. Hawkins, alias Willams, 34, married, Shelbourne, Nova Scotia.

"G. W. Clay, coloured, 28, married, City."

And so on, and so on. Great lumps were rising in Harvey's

throat, and his stomach reminded him of the day when he fell from the liner.

"May 10th.—Schooner *We 're Here* [the blood tingled all over him]. Otto Svendson, 20, single, City, lost overboard."

Once more a low, tearing cry from somewhere at the back of the hall.

"She should n't ha' come. She should n't ha' come," said Long Jack, with a cluck of pity.

"Don't scrowge, Harve," grunted Dan. Harvey heard that much, but the rest was all darkness spotted with fiery wheels. Disko leaned forward and spoke to his wife, where she sat with one arm round Mrs. Cheyne, and the other holding down the snatching, catching, ringed hands.

"Lean your head daown—right daown!" she whispered. "It 'll go off in a minute."

"I ca-an't! I do-don't! Oh, let me——" Mrs. Cheyne did not at all know what she said.

"You must," Mrs. Troop repeated. "Your boy 's jest fainted dead away. They do that some when they 're gettin' their growth. 'Wish to tend to him? We can git aout this side. Quite quiet. You come right along with me. Psha', my dear, we 're both women, I guess. We must tend to aour men-folk. Come!"

The *We 're Heres* promptly went through the crowd as a body-guard, and it was a very white and shaken Harvey that they propped up on a bench in an anteroom.

"Favours his ma," was Mrs. Troop's only comment, as the mother bent over her boy.

"How d' you suppose he could ever stand it?" she cried indignantly to Cheyne, who had said nothing at all. "It was horrible—horrible! We should n't have come. It 's wrong and wicked! It—it is n't right! Why—why could n't they put these things in the papers, where they belong? Are you better, darling?"

That made Harvey very properly ashamed. "Oh, I 'm all right, I guess," he said, struggling to his feet, with a broken giggle. "Must ha' been something I ate for breakfast."

"Coffee, perhaps," said Cheyne, whose face was all in

hard lines, as though it had been cut out of bronze. "We won't go back again."

"Guess 't would be 'baout 's well to git daown to the wharf," said Disko. "It 's close in along with them Dagoes, an' the fresh air will fresh Mrs. Cheyne up."

Harvey announced that he never felt better in his life; but it was not till he saw the *We 're Here*, fresh from the lumper's hands, at Wouverman's wharf, that he lost his all-overish feelings in a queer mixture of pride and sorrowfulness. Other people—summer boarders and such-like—played about in cat-boats or looked at the sea from pierheads; but he understood things from the inside—more things than he could begin to think about. None the less, he could have sat down and howled because the little schooner was going off. Mrs. Cheyne simply cried and cried every step of the way and said most extraordinary things to Mrs. Troop, who "babied" her till Dan, who had not been "babied" since he was six, whistled aloud.

And so the old crowd—Harvey felt like the most ancient of mariners—dropped into the old schooner among the battered dories, while Harvey slipped the stern-fast from the pier-head, and they slid her along the wharfside with their hands. Every one wanted to say so much that no one said anything in particular. Harvey bade Dan take care of Uncle Salters's sea-boots and Penn's doryanchor, and Long Jack entreated Harvey to remember his lessons in seamanship; but the jokes fell flat in the presence of the two women, and it is hard to be funny with green harbour-water widening between good friends.

"Up jib and fores'l!" shouted Disko, getting to the wheel, as the wind took her. "'See you later, Harve. Dunno but I come near thinkin' a heap o' you an' your folks."

Then she glided beyond ear-shot, and they sat down to watch her up the harbour. And still Mrs. Cheyne wept.

"Psha', my dear," said Mrs. Troop: "we 're both women, I guess. Like 's not it 'll ease your heart to hev your cry aout. God He knows it never done me a mite o' good, but then He knows I 've had something to cry fer!"

Now it was a few years later, and upon the other edge of America, that a young man came through the clammy sea fog up a windy street which is flanked with most expensive houses built of wood to imitate stone. To him, as he was standing by a hammered iron gate, entered on horseback—and the horse would have been cheap at a thousand dollars—another young man. And this is what they said:

"Hello, Dan!"

"Hello, Harve!"

"What 's the best with you?"

"Well, I 'm so 's to be that kind o' animal called second mate this trip. Ain't you most through with that triple-invoiced college of yours?"

"Getting that way. I tell you, the Leland Stanford Junior, is n't a circumstance to the old *We 're Here;* but I 'm coming into the business for keeps next fall."

"Meanin' aour packets?"

"Nothing else. You just wait till I get my knife into you, Dan. I 'm going to make the old line lie down and cry when I take hold."

"I 'll resk it," said Dan, with a brotherly grin, as Harvey dismounted and asked whether he were coming in.

"That 's what I took the cable fer; but, say, is the doctor anywheres araound? I 'll draown that crazy nigger some day, his one cussed joke an' all."

There was a low, triumphant chuckle, as the ex-cook of the *We 're Here* came out of the fog to take the horse's bridle. He allowed no one but himself to attend to any of Harvey's wants.

"Thick as the Banks, ain't it, doctor?" said Dan, propitiatingly.

But the coal-black Celt with the second-sight did not see fit to reply till he had tapped Dan on the shoulder, and for the twentieth time croaked the old, old prophecy in his ear.

"Master—man. Man—master," said he. "You remember, Dan Troop, what I said? On the *We 're Here?*"

"Well, I won't go so far as to deny that it do look like it as things stand at present," said Dan. "She was a noble packet, and one way an' another I owe her a heap—her and Dad."

"Me too," quoth Harvey Cheyne.

# UNFORGETTABLE
# READING

**THE INCREDIBLE JOURNEY by SHEILA BURNFORD.** The heart warming story of a Labrador retriever, a bull terrier and a Siamese cat and their epic journey across the Canadian wilderness in the dead of winter to return to the family they love. 50c ☐

**APRIL MORNING by HOWARD FAST.** The exciting story of a young boy living in revolutionary America who suddenly becomes a man during the battle of Lexington. 60c ☐